MW01016100

POLICE

Selected Issues
in
Canadian Law
Enforcement

POLICE

Selected Issues in Canadian Law Enforcement

Edited by

Dennis Forcese

Rideau Series no. 3

The Golden Dog Press
Ottawa – Canada – 2002

Copyright © 2002 by Individual Authors.

ISBN 0-919614-91-4

All rights reserved. No part of this publication — other than in brief form for review or scholarly purposes — may be reproduced, stored in a retrieval system, or transmitted, in any form or by any means, electronic, mechanical, photocopying, recording or otherwise, without the prior permission of the copyright holders.

Canadian Cataloguing in Publication Data

Police : selected issues in Canadian Law enforcement / edited by Dennis P. Forcese

(Rideau series ; 3)
Includes bibliographical references.
ISBN 0-919614-91-4

    1. Police — Canada.   I. Forcese, Dennis, 1941 – II. Series.

HV8157.P63 2002   363.2′0971   C2002-902280-0

Cover design by The Dundurn Group of Toronto.

Typesetting by Carleton Production Centre of Nepean.

Printed in Canada.

Published by:

    The Golden Dog Press is an imprint of Haymax Inc.,
    P.O. Box 393, Kemptville, Ont., K0G 1J0 Canada

The Golden Dog Press wishes to express its appreciation to the Canada Council and the Ontario Arts Council for the support these Councils have extended to its publishing programme.

Contents

Introduction

This book is an anthology and not a monograph. Each of the chapters was written as an essay, sometimes by the author alone and sometimes by or with students and colleagues. The style and content differ, from literature review, news analysis, and survey data, but there is a relationship among the essays. The relationship is imperfectly captured by the word "issues" in the book title. Although there are many issues related to Canadian policing unaddressed in this volume, each of the essays takes up a topic selected as noteworthy by the author. There is also a thematic flow and interdependence, linked by discussion of change and community policing.

Chapter One locates Canadian policing within a nation-building context. The issue may be distinguished as the role of police in a democratic society. The integral role of police in the history of the Canadian nation, securing a frontier, and supporting an evolving public order, is outlined. The essay stresses the unique contribution of Canadian police to the democratic social fabric. This theme becomes all the more relevant as context for some consideration of post-September 11, 2001 developments in policing, pondered in the book's concluding essay.

Chapter Two takes up the question or issue of a changing police role as Canadian society itself has altered, with massive urbanisation and multicultural and multiracial immigration. The ideology of change in Canadian police is vested in an imported and imperfect concept: community policing. The chapter attempts to locate this concept within a brief historical and policy context, and especially the realisation that community policing was a response to a crisis in police work and public confidence in the United States — a crisis that was not experienced in Canada.

Finding agreement on the systemic components of community policing is considered an issue in Chapter Three. Because of the imprecision associated with community policing — an ab-

sence of consensus as to what it is conceptually, let alone operationally—the chapter attempts a sort of checklist or template
of community policing components. This is done with the understanding that community policing is customised policing, and
there is no "one size fits all." The discussion is also embedded in
the view that much of what is represented as community policing
is not at all adequate to the concept or theory but rather, is often
a public relations overlay upon the persisting traditional structure and practices of police organisations. Many so-called community policing measures introduced have been trivial, involving
a small minority of personnel, and have rightly passed unnoticed
by the public.

Information gathering is pondered in Chapter Four as fundamental to all policing. Policing is understood by many, perhaps
most especially critics, as a trade in information. In this essay
the issue is that of adequate information use and analysis, especially in a shift to community policing. The classic difficulty
of all large bureaucratic organisations is the task of optimally
collecting, analyzing, disseminating, and using intelligence in a
timely manner. If anything, this demand upon police organisations is underlined in the months since September 2001 and the
extensive attention to terrorism. Community policing has been,
in part, an attempt to better ground police officers in communities, the resulting enhanced information contrasting with that
available from remote policing. Yet, information needs transcend
local community boundaries, and information gathering, coordination, and analysis within the larger organisation arguably are
more difficul with decentralised community policing.

Also an issue with the public and with employees has been
organisational merger. Whether it be public sectors such as local
government, health care, education, or policing, there is a prevalent senior government assumption that bigger is better and more
efficient. While community policing has ostensibly been the agenda
of change the more familiar government agenda has been larger
police services. The regional concept has featured in Ontario, Quebec, and New Brunswick, introducing organisational impediments
to community policing. The merits of regional mergers are pondered in Chapter Five.

Another of the conspicuous obstacles to community policing in Canada has been the attitude of employee groups. Policing
historically has been resistant to any change other than technological. People working in policing, at all ranks, prefer to work in
the manner which they know. The familiar, the routinised, the con-

trollable are inevitably deemed preferable to change, especially if that change — as in the case of community policing — appears to require a different skill set, additional responsibilities, and perhaps too, a less romanticised image of policing. Police associations, protecting job conditions vested in collective agreements, have not embraced the prospect of community policing, unconvinced of the alleged benefits such as greater job satisfaction. But also, they have resisted community policing in part because the associated changes have been seen as top–down, that is, management initiatives not vested in prior consultations and consensus.

The theme of police associations as a countervails to change, and as an increasingly politicised police body generally challenging managerial discretion, is briefly illustrated in Chapter Six. This essay is admittedly focussing upon a somewhat atypical police association, Toronto, which has adopted a peculiarly adversarial and political style. The extreme instance of Toronto, however, illustrates that a police organisation, police culture, and the nature and quality of police relations with the public are not simply functions of the organisation chart and of management actions. Police associations can powerfully shape the environment and image of police.

Also featuring prominently in policing over the past few decades have been special paramilitary units within policing, which we may summarily refer to as tactical units. Chapter Seven presents some basic and unique information from the 1990s on the extent to which tactical units have become a normal feature of Canadian policing. Whether full- or part-time, specialising in crowd control or emergency response or high-risk call-outs, these teams have come to be very prestigious paramilitary units within policing. At a time when policing was supposed to be showing a kinder and gentler side by way of community-sensitive reorganisation and service, tactical units have represented an emphasis upon high-impact forceful policing — in action and even symbolically, given their uniform gear. Just when policing is to have been shifting to prevention, these units represent a turn to impact policing, with officers often engaged in regular patrol and statistically known to be responding to more and more calls formerly handled by regular officers. As well, as ever more females are being integrated into the diverse roles of policing, the tactical units have remained male preserves.

In fact, it has been suggested that an adaptation of police organisations to increased female participation has been the creation of such specialised units for men, as more and more women find themselves remaining in patrol. While the now-common experience of women in regular policing is an undoubted major development, what has remained unfulfilled is a progression through the rank hierarchy as well as into special units. Chapter Eight examines some basic information from the late 1990s relating to the experience of women as police officers.

The police officer as worker faces many occupational challenges, from the unchanging core of police duty associated with routinised work interrupted by periodic danger, to the unremitting demands of working within a bureaucratic command hierarchy. It is remarkable that police organisations have not better attended to police stress. Very spotty support programs exist among Canadian police services and the issue of stress tends to remain a police dirty secret. A very imperfect literature exists on the manifestations and consequences of stress among police officers, such as burnout, suicide, alcoholism, and marital breakdown. In Canada in particular much of the information available is merely anecdotal. Marriage generally has been assumed to be an area of difficulty due to shift work and the intense isolation of the job. Periodically, for example, reports of domestic abuse by police officers surface (*New York Times*, "Domestic Abuse Complaints Against Officers are on the Rise," November 14, 1999), sometimes as feature popular press articles (for example, Alex Roslin, "Black and Blue," *Saturday Night*, September 23, 2000). Chapter Nine looks at police and the marital relationship.

Finally we conclude with musings in Chapter Ten. What does the future hold for policing? Especially, what does the future hold in light of the consequences of September 11, 2001? The generally persisting issues associated with balancing citizens' rights and police powers, and the correct role of police in a democratic society contending with international threats, serves to bring us full circle from our discussions in Chapter One.

DPF

January, 2002

One

Policing and Nation Building

Dennis Forcese

Introduction

In the evolving democratic and legal culture of any society, an important element is that of front-line social control. Public police have been integral to the civil order and character of Canadian society. They have been a policy instrument of national development, and therefore a vital arm of the state beyond the visible functions of crime control. They have also served to represent the "impersonality" (Podgorecki, 1995) and legitimacy of the justice system. The "objective" or "legalistic" (Wilson, 1978) style of Royal Canadian Mounted policing and major municipal policing have been almost an ideal–typical representation of impersonal application of law. The Canadian police have served practical and symbolic functions, legitimating impersonal law. They have been chartered and regulated by senior governments, bound by legislation and by contract, and have represented and acted for the Canadian democratic nation state.

Historic Development

In order to generalise about law enforcement and the development of civil society a rather familiar history may be summarised. Canada's national development, formally demarcated in 1867 with the British North America Act, set in train a socio-political experiment that differed from that of the United States. A small population of fewer than 5 million, divided by language and cultural origin (French and English), fending off American expansionism, and dispersed over the larger part of the North American continent, established a stable society vested in rule of law, and commitment to "peace, order and good government."

Canada is a deliberate rather than a populist national con-

5

struct. British legislation, the British North America Act, founded the new and unlikely federal state in 1867. The nation was not founded in revolution nor in tribal or ethnic homogeneity. Rather, colonial remnants of populations, scattered from the East coast of northern America to the Great Lakes, deliberately entered a political contract intended to secure from American national expansion the northern half of the continent, from coast to coast. Lipset (1963) has written of the United States as the "first new nation." In loyalist anti-republican counterpoint to the American, Canada was another national experiment.

The inaugural government of John A. MacDonald conceived a "National Policy" of deliberate state-managed national development. The concept of "state capitalism" aptly captures an historic Canadian government role, as in construction of transporation and communications systems in the "national interest" (Panitch, 1977). The federal government engaged in massive developmental enterprises, from the railroad to national energy projects, and later health care. The National Policy also depended upon implementation of law and order. Claims to sovereignty over scantly populated and contested frontier territories and the aborignal populations residing there had to be established. A direct agent of such policy was the state police, the (Royal) Northwest Mounted Police, operating by 1873 and dispatched to the western frontier well in advance of population migration. Unlike the United States, by the time traders and especially settlers arrived, characteristically there was in place a prior police presence and law enforcement.

In the course of Canadian national history, the population changed dramatically, becoming progressively more heterogeneous, with massive European immigration and considerable transborder migration to and from the United States. In the course of this population mobility, including settlement of frontier territories in the West and the North, the legislative authority of the federal parliament and of provincial legislatures was represented and enforced by police forces.

This initial Canadian policing model had origins in a colonial police model. That is, the Northwest Mounted Police (to become the Royal Northwest and then the Royal Canadian Mounted Police) was the direct agent of the federal state, legislatively defined and mandated by the federal Parliament, and was modelled organisationally on the British colonial paramilitary forces, most particularly, the Royal Irish Constabulary. The NWMP secured the Western frontier, dealing with traders, native populations, and the incursions of adventurers from the United States, in advance of population migration and settlement. Similarly, in provincial hinterlands, provincial police services — state police — acted to secure frontier expansion, as with the Ontario Provincial Police.

Police enforcement in wilderness and frontier territories, as an impersonal agent of government and law, contrasted with the American frontier experience. In the United States, law, policing, and order lagged behind settlement. The frontier was initially appropriated by adventurers and large landowners. Law enforcement (gunfighters, bounty hunters, vigilantes) was itself a form of "free enterprise." When American migrants contested territory with aboriginal populations or earlier colonial settlers, the American military were called upon. In Canada the NWMP was, depite its marked paramilitary character, a civil and not a military force. Unlike the United States' military in the frontier, the NWMP engaged in peacekeeping and not warfare, in nation-building and not conquest.

It is instructive to peruse early historical texts to find an explicit record of intent. Haydon (1973:19), originally published in 1910, writes that "the North-West Mounted Police was to be purely a civil force, like the Royal Irish Constabulary." It and its members were not bound by the Queen's regulations but rather by statute of the Parliament of Canada, the Dominion Statute. To further illustrate the intent and perception of the police role in national development is Haydon's observation that their "advent into the western provinces was to herald a new era of peace and prosperity" (1973:16).

Police presence effected not only control and sovereignty but also fixed a legal ethic. The intercession of the police was, in effect, an expression of the formal/rational application of state bureaucracy. Not only was direct control achieved but also a culture of order and rule of law. In contrast to the more "free-booting" style of the United States, Canada experienced controlled settlement and social development. The limits of conduct, and the nature of deviance and crime, were explicitly understood and accepted.

While the state police, the NWMP, were securing the frontier, in the more populous central and eastern Canadian towns, another form of policing emerged, influenced by the model of the London Metropolitan Police. Municipal police forces existed before Confederation, and evolved rapidly thereafter. The municipal police forces were defined and regulated by provincial legislation. Statutory authority and limitations, and civilian control, were explicit. As modelled by Ontario, civil control was vested in a Police Act and subject to civilian oversight by government-appointed civilian police commissions; elsewhere, civil control was directly by municipal councils.

Unlike municipal police in the United States, there was not a prevalent public perception or practice of the police as agents of political immigrant interests, such as the Irish in New York City. Therefore, too, there was not the profound gulf between social classes — the American view of public police as a working class gang and private police for the privileged. Through the history of the Canadian nation the police have enjoyed exceptionally high prestige and trust among the public. In the United States police have tended to be perceived as agents of politically organised immigrant and working-class interests. Somewhat like the British "bobbie" — and quite unlike the American police officer — the Canadian police officer, and especially the RCMP officer, was a symbol of decorum and propriety, even as recruits were often immigrants of the working class.

The symbolic and soon romanticised role of the NWMP/RCMP served a significant legitimation function through Canadian history. There was also a "halo effect" for other police forces in Canada. The municipal police forces, even as they were engaged in relatively mundane local control functions, benefitted from the "halo effect" of the romantic imagery associated with the state police. Public regard and compliance were normal.

In the populous old settled provinces of Quebec and Ontario the NWMP was not the overt police presence; instead, locally organised municipal police, and eventually, provincial versions of state police (the Ontario Provincial Police and the Quebec Provincial Police, presently the Sûreté du Québec), engaged in day-to-day law enforcement. Like the NWMP, the OPP and QPP also had a frontier role, policing the rural hinterland of each of these massive provinces but, following from comparable legislation, responsible to provincial legislatures and not the federal government. One can recognise in these provincial police agencies another tactic in the checks and balances of Canadian national development as a federal state.

Also, insofar as generalising the impact of policing, although the original objective of the NWMP was frontier policing, the statute did allow the NWMP to serve as a national police force. As the RCMP role expanded from frontier policing to other government-required actions (such as alcohol enforcement, a major element of the role of the RCMP in the Atlantic provinces) and to contract-based local municipal policing in provinces other than Ontario and

Quebec, the romance of RCM policing, and their repute as objective and fair agents of impersonal law, carried over. RCMP "legalistic" (Wilson, 1978) policing was viewed as the model of police professionalism and impersonal law enforcement.

Ericson (1981) has written of the role of contemporary police in "making crime" by virtue of the offences and offenders to which they choose to attend. But the converse is, of course, equally true: that the police define the nature of civil order. In Canada, the explicit and systematic application of bureaucratic state nation building through the agencies of objective policing have contributed to a Canadian culture of order and respect for law. But in the process, reflecting this "culture," the police, at least the RCMP, themselves have became a symbol of Canadian nationhood and a symbol of state legitimation.

A concept of police objectivity and political neutrality was in fact specified in police acts. Historically the policing role was itself checked, always subordinate to parliament, legislature, civil definition vested in legislation, and local civilian control. Characteristically police legislation also insisted that police personnel, unlike virtually any other citizens, be political non-participants. In Canada the police distance from political action has historically been much more pronounced than in the United States. As an "essential service," here quite similar to the American experience, only belatedly and grudgingly have police been accorded the right of employee association, and usually not the right to affiliate and to strike (Forcese, 1980, 1999). While Canadian police, therefore, have traditionally been accorded a high degree of operational discretion, they have nonetheless remained subject to effective government control.

With civil accountability in place and a shared set of legal norms with the public, Canadian police historically were afforded a great latitude. Police discretion explicitly was acknowledged and encouraged (Grosman, 1975). There was less tendency, outside of founding legislation, to rule-bind the police in Canada, and a high level of judicial confidence in police evidence. Even illegally obtained evidence was tolerated.

Consistent, too, with public confidence and police discretion, the police had been expected to — and did — police themselves. Major crises of police misconduct, as have been prevalent in the United States, did not and still do not feature hugely in Canadian policing, reinforcing the positively perceived association of policing and law that led to great respect and compliance with the police.

With municipal police forces increasingly in place, and the national policy of sovereignty and expansion achieved, by approximately the time of World War I, the federal government harboured notions that the RNWMP had served its function and could be disbanded. A decision had apparently been reached to do so. But in this period, in Canada as in other nations, significant labour organising and job actions were occurring; police intervention in industrial disputes had become a conspicuous new role. However, governments had some suspicions of the reliability of local municipal police personnel. In particular, with the Winnipeg General Strike of 1919, the Winnipeg municipal police also went out on strike. The provincial and federal governments had a perception of imminent chaos and revolution; the RNWMP police were sent in and were instrumental in breaking the general strike. Their future was thereby secured as being a reliable agent of the state. To the present date, as tested in the Supreme Court of Canada, the RCMP, Canada's largest police service, is the only service whose members do not have an employee organisation — that is, a union.

Thereafter, redefined in new legislation as the Royal Canadian Mounted Police, the "Mounties" adapted to the twentieth century by increasingly doing municipal policing. This represented another expression of legal evolution within the federation. The RCMP, a federal police service, entered into contract relationships with provincial and municipal governments to provide policing services.

Legitimacy Challenged

Police unionism may be seen as a fissure in the effective affiliation of the state, law, and the police early in the twentieth century when municipal police began to create employee organisations. Initially these initiatives were met with distrust by the civil authorities, as they had been in Britain, the United States, Australia, and elsewhere; to protect state interests, the Canadian federal state and provinces rediscovered the usefulness of police responsible to senior governments. To the present, police unions are viewed with suspicion, and little disruption or impropriety is required to generate a sense of unionised police violating a relationship of trust with the public.

Further erosion developed in the historic legitimation role of police in the 1980s. The Canadian Charter of Rights (1982), and later legislation in provinces such as Ontario (Police Services Act 1993), served to limit the discretion of the police, and called into

10

question their position as impartial agents of impartial law. Where Canadian legal tradition had been comfortably entwined with the role of civil policing, the 1990s witnessed a more aggressive state intervention in police conduct. More overt formal restraints upon police conduct were introduced, along with more formal mechanisms of police regulation and accountability. The state effected American-style control mechanisms upon police conduct to supplement traditional legislative restraint and contract restraint — devices such as investigations units and civilian review boards. In so doing, we may speculate that the state eroded the affirmative mythology, legitimacy, and effectiveness of the police as an agent of state policy and rule of law, just as police associations have done.

Historically in Ontario, as elsewhere in Canada, the direct control of the state and the well-established legitimation of police operations, had permitted police forces to police themselves. But in Ontario the 1993 legislation called for uniform public complaints procedures, mandatory investigation in specified circumstances by a special investigations unit, a public complaints commissioner and bureau, and civilian boards of inquiry. All of these were in addition to internal investigations, and accountability and responsibility of police service boards or commissions and the government itself. In a sense, in effecting such measures, the police were being detached somewhat from their previous status as the direct arm of legitimate state function and symbolic agent of legal culture or norms. They were, for the first time historically in Canada, being represented as somewhat suspect — just like their American colleagues.

While much of this oversight structure was subsequently removed by a Progressive Conversative government in one province, Ontario, an investigative unit (Special Investigations Unit, SIU) has remained in place over the objections of the police associations, and arguably has tended to subvert, along with press reports, the high moral ground historically occupied by the police in the public eye.

Additionally Canadian police services, like police in other societies, have in the 1990s embraced the vague concept of community policing, implying a more localised and community-responsive form of policing, in contrast to the state-central ideal form of policing that has characterised the Canadian historical experience. In some part, just as with the introduction of investigation units and even civilian review bodies for complaints against police, community policing may be seen as an attempt to respond to greater population diversity and some breakdown in the socio-legal normative consensus that police had helped create. The localism of community policing is contradictory of, even an expression of non-confidence in, the historic Canadian representation of law as non-particular, as it incorporates community-relative conceptions of enforcement standards and priorities.

Since the 1990s, Canadian police have embarked upon an amended presentation of self: community-based. The concept of community policing currently infuses any discussion of police services in Canada, as it does in the United States and Western Europe. In Ontario, Canada's most populous and heterogeneous province, community policing is effectively required by statute, imprecisely embedded in the Police Services Act. At the outset of the Act is stated "The need for co-operation between the providers of police services and the communities they serve." Also specified is "The need to ensure that police forces are representative of the communities they serve." For example, Metropolitan Toronto — the destination of almost two-thirds of all immigrants to Canada, the largest metropolis in the country, with the largest municipal police service — has been obliged, along with every jurisdiction in the province, to implement community policing, even as the statute leaves the expectation unspecified. Similarly, while not referenced in the federal RCMP Act, under the authority of its Commissioner the mission statement of the Royal Canadian Mounted Police specifies "community policing" as a policy commitment.

One observer (Friedmann, 1992) marvels that the concept of community policing and related reform attempts should be so prevalent in Canada, adopted in the absence of major crises in policing. Yet, in Canada, as elsewhere, there is a relationship between perceived crises and community-based policing reform, most particularly deriving from a succession of incidents of alleged abuse of police power, including deadly force, involving minority populations of third world origins. In Toronto, as in Montreal, such incidents involving Black residents have led to inquests, and to consultant and commission reports, while in Quebec and in Western Canada police encounters with aboriginal persons in and out of cities have similarly been sensational challenges to the traditionally sanguine and trusting Canadian confidence in the police. As the objectivity and competence of police services in a society of increasingly evident ethnic and racial diversity were called into question, the reform promised by the happy notion of community policing, an import like many others from the United States, was available for adoption, and easily mandated by state authorities.

The coincidence of severe public sector budget stress additionally spurred an inclination to seek or at least pose for reform as a means of regaining, or more accurately, retaining public confidence. Polling data continue to suggest that the police remain well regarded by the large majority of the Canadian public, even as this high regard is not shared by some minority populations.

From the inception of the Canadian nation and throughout its history, state intervention in the public interest has been featured and approved as being as in the public interest; police interventions were similarly expected and respected. State and police were conceded to be collaborative, with the police as an apolitical arm of legitimate state policy. In contrast to the United States where police were seen to be local, parochial, and interest-bound, police in Canada contributed to national development and earned a legitimacy by virtue of association with senior governments. In the United States, therefore, community policing as a philosophy and model was truly reformist, an attempt to establish a local basis of legitimacy, whereas in Canada the police by and large had no such extreme need, even as there were changing social circumstances.

The expectations apparently associated with community policing, such as improved public satisfaction and confidence, improved allocation of resources in a manner consonant with public needs and expectations, and improved crime prevention and enforcement, are conceded to depend upon co-ordinated public agency responses to the social problems of an urbanised, mobile, heterogeneous population. Curiously the Canadian police appear to have bought and adopted as their own the argument that they are at the limits of conventional enforcement and prevention. Having propagated this view the police are being obliged, de facto, to assume a leadership role in this coordination, a role for which they are exceedingly ill-prepared (Horn, 1991:129). Police are being challenged to be more open, more collaborative, yet more professional (Sparrow et al., 1990). Somewhat ironically but inevitably, as police services promise to accept the more or less explicit invitation to assume a leadership role and to be service-, information-, and policy-proactive in their communities, they open themselves to new criticisms, or at least, new versions of old criticisms, especially if they fail to deliver conspicuous benefits.

Sceptics (Ericson and Haggerty, 1997) claim that community policing promises to be but another hollow panacea, marginally expressed in substantive reform or change in police organisation and practices, and ultimately simply another means for police to control the law enforcement agenda with a view to organisational maintenance, budgets, and disarming of critics. Even advocates will acknowledge that the concept is vague, shifty, all-encompassing, and "elusive" (Friedmann, 1992:2–3), and means different things to different people — perhaps more importantly, it means what area police services say they are doing. Also a class bias may be remarked, as police "community" collaboration is effected with relatively stable and conforming middle-class populations, and not with the urban segments historically associated with intensive police activity.

In attempting a shift to community policing, in effect mandated by the state and police managers, there has been indifferent public response, and some marked police employee group resistance. Police collective agreements, a legal counterpoint to police acts, have provided impediments to the historic state steering of police agencies. Police unions have been suspicious of the workload implications of community policing, and of the prospect of job-displacing civilian volunteers. Additionally the collective agreements negotiated by these associations have fixed new legal parameters for policing, but more significantly, have de-romanticised police as effective agents of impersonal law.

Conclusions

In summary, Canadian historical experience is offered as an instance in which impersonal law was effected, originating in deliberate political contract, but implemented, reinforced, and legitimated by police agencies. The legal culture established, and the society subject to new tensions, the police role in representing the integrity and character of law, is gradually seen to have eroded. While the Canadian police themselves remain subject to rather effective legal constraint, as has historically been the case, their status as arbitrators and representatives of impersonal law and justice is diminishing.

Through the 1990s, and even earlier, the police role in relationship to law and state legitimacy was changing. The police could be seen to be increasingly disassociated from the state and abstract conceptions of justice, rule of law, and legitimacy. Current practices have de-mystified Canadian police, and appear to be rendering them less powerful as instruments of legitimation and impersonal law. These alterations include more aggressive and explicit policy criticisms by public sector bodies and government, and increasingly elaborate state-legislated mechanisms of police conduct review and investigation. As well, police job actions and aggressive police unions have further amended historical Canadian conceptions of the police insofar as public notions of an objective police role. Also, it may even be that the affirmative innovations of community policing, stressing local affiliations and a more relative conception of legal and enforcement priorities, comprise a reform that is amending the traditional efficacy of the police as an agent of the state and as a symbol of impersonal law.

No longer the paragons of lawful virtue, the Canadian police are increasingly being viewed by Canadians as very imperfect rather than impartial agents of the state, and a powerful self-serving interest group. The 1990s may have marked the end of what had been a Canadian police function: legitimating as well as enforcing the law. It is yet to be seen whether genuine problem-oriented community policing will be throughly implemented in Canadian police services as a new legitimation device. Alternately, it is yet to be seen whether the terrorist events of September 2001, resulting in an immediate affirmation of more interventionist policing roles, will alter this "modern" distancing of the state from policing, and result in a reinforcement of an historically explicit affiliation of policing as a vital arm of senior governments and the Canadian polity.

Two

Origins of Community Policing

Nancy Morris and Dennis Forcese

Introduction

It is commonplace to acknowledge that municipal policing in North America had its origins in Sir Robert Peel's conception of the London Metropolitan Police in 1829. Particularly in the past two decades, as community policing has been promoted, Peel's "principles of policing" have been trotted out and invoked as a thoroughly modern approach to policing. This chapter is a brief review of the present ostensible infatuation with community policing. The theme becomes, in a sense, back to the future, as community policing is rediscovered in the nineteenth-century origins of modern policing and embraced by American reformers seeking to re-energise and legitimise policing. Moreover, the past may be seen as the present and future, too, in that quite possibly we are witnessing the principles of community policing dissipating in the face of organisational and social exigencies, just as the principles of Sir Robert Peel had.

Origins of Community Policing

In colonial Canada, as remarked in the previous chapter, policing developed with roots vested in Peel's Royal Irish Constabulary (the explicit para-military character of the North West Mounted Police) and in Peel's London municipal police model of an empowered subset of the general citizenry. A sense of accountability to the civilian authority was a feature of both models, although the municipal London model in effect came to be far more reactive than Peel had envisioned. In Canada the early municipal police were soon in uniforms as in England, despite military connotations, but unlike in England, they were armed. And as in England, by and large they were charged with maintaining public order rather

16

more than dealing with major crime: policing taverns was enormously more prevalent than apprehending criminals. Policing was viewed as a respectable trade, and not a profession, and therefore suited to working-class people, often immigrants, who then worked within a para-military command structure.

Through much of history traditional policing was incident-focussed and reactive, with relatively scant regard to analysis or even effectiveness (Leighton and Mitzak, 1991:1-9). Internal organisation command was emphasised over officer responsibility, and increasingly police became remote from the communities they served. Technology as much as command attitude impacted this distancing, as did urban sprawl, with the automobile and radio communications taking officers off the streets and away from routine contacts with the public. Direct interaction between public and the police came increasingly to be confined to situations of police response and situations of trouble, rather than benign interactions, thereby distorting police attitudes of the public and vice versa.

Moreover, as the automobile from the 1920s steadily replaced foot patrol, and as two-way radios permitted increased supervision of patrol officers as well as more rapid crime calls, policing began to move away from an emphasis on social order to one of crime-fighting. The police role came to be defined in terms of numbers of calls answered, response time, and number of arrests made. "Professionalism came to mean a combination of managerial efficiency, technological sophistication, and an emphasis on crime-fighting" rather than social service (Peak and Glensor, 1996:10). The police became ever more alienated and cut off from the supportive public — a vital source of information necessary for preventing and solving crime and the basis of legitimation of the policing role. Even as the police officer was poorly educated and ill-trained, in the United States especially police expertise or professionalism was invoked, and taken to mean hierarchical managerial control and the ability to impact crime. Additionally, as probably exemplified by the RCMP, professionalism was taken to mean a distancing from community ties in the name of objectivity and impartial treatment, a style that translated into a powerful legitimacy. Yet it was also perceived, at least in the United States, that the professional model of policing was failing (Peak and Glensor, 1996:14-15). Crime rates and public fear were rising, and in the more heterogeneous North American societies of the 1960s, it was evident that minority citizens did not perceive police as favorably as the more privileged, and in Canada, as the citizen majority

17

had done historically.

The United States

Perhaps because of growing population diversity and urbanisation, as early as the 1950s there was increasing interest in amending police–community relations in the United States, which soon spilled over into Canada and other nations. While community relations units had become prevalent, and were generally viewed as marginal within the dominant police culture, alternate service models eventually came to be mooted — concepts such as team policing, neighborhood foot patrol, preventive policing, problem-oriented policing, community-based policing (Morris, 1997:35–40).

It is difficult to reconstruct the modern origins of the community policing concept, but probably much of the credit can be attached to Louis Radelet and Herman Goldstein. At Michigan State University in the 1950s where Louis Radelet founded and operated the National Institute on Police and Community Relations (Peak and Glensor, 1996: 13), police and other community leaders met annually at the institute's 5-day conferences. "In some years, more than 600 participants came from as many as 165 communities and 30 states and several foreign countries" (Radelet and Carter, 1994:24). The institute programs included emphasis upon re-focussing police upon prevention, encouraging police–citizen partnerships, improved police–community communication and understanding, and inter-professional approaches to prevention and problem-solving (Radelet and Carter, 1994).

By 1979 Herman Goldstein was proposing something that he called "problem-oriented policing," as methodically presented in his book. His approach sought "a better balance between the reactive and the proactive aspects of policing" and more effective use of rank-and-file officers (Goldstein, 1990: 3, 32). The approach was to stress interaction with the community, and to be "holistic" or comprehensive in its policing style. Incidents were to be grouped, and the substantive problems underlying the incidents were to be addressed and solved on a customised basis in collaboration with communities.

Notable experiments in community or problem-oriented policing were undertaken in the United States. A noteworthy example was a foot patrol initiative in Flint, Michigan (1979). Officers helped establish community associations, from which they solicited input into policing priorities and programs. They used liaison, referrals, and interventions to provide services beyond their law enforcement duties. Among the results, citizens felt safer, and officers experienced greater job satisfaction (Trojanowicz, 1986:96-106).

In 1984 in Brooklyn, New York, a Community Patrol Officer Program (CPOP) was introduced. As in Flint, the project was intended to attempt foot patrol and non-traditional services in addition to law enforcement. Officers were expected to help organise community groups and to work with the community in problem-solving. The subsequent level of public satisfaction led to the elaboration of the program in six additional precincts in 1985, and all precincts by 1988 (McElroy, Cosgrove and Sadd, 1993:194-196).

Canada

By the 1990s the mantra of community policing was prevalent in Canada. Yet, even as there were a few zealous advocates, such as out of Edmonton, there seemed no evident crises or policy push towards such reform. As Friedmann (1992:99) remarked, "What is interesting about Canadian policing ... is that despite the relative lack of external pressures for police reform the country has gradually adopted a shift towards community policing." Or, to insert a note of critical reserve, one might say "has gradually adopted" the rhetoric and overlay of community policing.

In some part one can detect a typical Canadian top-down context for the emergence of community policing. The resort to a community policing model was a deliberate policy decision of senior governments, with the state, therefore, continuing in Canada its close affiliation with policing, even as it sought to shift its ideology and legitimation away from central control to local representativeness and accountability. "During the 1960s and early 1970s, influenced by bureaucrats and consultants familiar with innovations in the United States, the Canadian government introduced a variety of programs with the general, if none the less vague, purpose of promoting citizen participation" (Loney, 1977:454).

In the late 1960s some federal government initiatives began to set the stage for citizens to have a greater role and more responsibility in the criminal justice system. The Ouimet Report of 1969 stressed a need, for example, for direct citizen participation in correctional services (cited in Sauve, 1977: 27). Another Task Force and Report, chaired by Judge Robert Sauve (Sauve, 1977), emerged in 1976 from prior consultations between the John Howard Society and the Solicitor General's Senior Policy Advisory Committee. These discussions had envisaged a sharing of responsibility

19

among levels of government, but especially noteworthy, the participation of "private sector and organised community interest groups ... in the field of criminal justice, including crime prevention, diversion and community education programs" (Sauve, 1977:28-29). In the case of the Sauve Task Force, a broad Canada-wide federal/provincial consultation ensued, with over five hundred "informed participants," from deputy ministers to community groups. The report called for broad citizen participation in the criminal justice system, including having "community groups ... design and develop their own responses to crime in their own communities" (Sauve, 1977:111-112).

In 1972 a newly created Ministry of the Solicitor General of Ontario was made responsible for the province's policing. The new Solicitor General quickly acted to establish a Task Force on Policing in Ontario. Premised upon changing social circumstances, including urbanisation, increasing police costs, and an apprehended breakdown in police relations with the public, the Task Force Report suggested basic changes (Hale, 1974:3-11) — changes that were to involve government, police commissions, police managers, and noteably, also police associations. Interestingly, again illustrating the top-down character of the drive to community policing, of the seventeen members of the Task Force, only five were members of the general public, while the remaining represented various provincial government and police organisations.

Congruent with this Ontario re-thinking, others in Canada were noting American innovations. A handful of senior police officers pioneered in seeking out American innovations. The Chief of Police of Victoria, B.C. became aware of the Detroit mini-stations initiated in 1974 and sent a constable to study and report back on the project. While still a Vancouver police sergeant, Chief Bill Snowdon had been in Ottawa at the Ministry of the Solicitor General and had learned about such innovations. As chief, he became an agent for change, pointing the way to community-based policing reform and elaborating a program of community stations in Victoria. The program emphasised a role for citizen volunteers and local crime prevention initiatives (Walker and Walker, 1989; Walker et al., 1992).

In the 1970s in Calgary, Chief Brian Sawyer attempted to decentralise and localise policing in distinguishable communities or neighbourhoods by way of city-wide zone policing. His initiative was embedded explicitly in the concepts of policing attributable to Peel; Sawyer spoke of crime prevention and becoming "people-oriented" (Calgary Police Service Annual Report, 1977). Presaging a symbolic change to come elsewhere in the country, his police agency was called a "service" and not a "force."

By the 1980s, more jurisdictions were climbing aboard the community-based reform bandwagon. The city of Halifax, in a top-down change initiated by the chief, implemented a system of zone policing (Clairmont, 1990). In Western Canada again, in 1987 a Neighbourhood Foot Patrol Programme was implemented in 21 neighbourhoods in Edmonton (Hornick et al., 1993:311). Subsequently, community stations became normative in the city, and a prominent Edmonton spokesman, Chris Braiden, came to be recognised as the "guru" of community policing in Canada. His rationale for community policing resonated, as he stressed that police would have to become better informed about their communities. Rather than develop mind-sets on the basis of service responses, the police needed to "start meeting normal people under normal circumstances on a regular basis" (Braiden, 1986:34–35).

Also in the 1980s the Canadian Police College began regularly to offer course content on community policing and crime prevention, and across the country, major police organisations began to implement programs serving to show that they too had "bought-in" to the new conceptual icon of police modernism, community policing. There was even legislated change, as the revised Ontario Police Services Act (1993) called for amending agency names to police *service* rather than force or department, and required the chief of police to ensure the provision of community-oriented services. Virtually all police service mission statements, including those of the RCMP, OPP, and the Quebec Sûreté as well as municipal police incorporated community policing as their model of intent.

Conclusions

The rhetoric, the philosophy, and some of the components of community policing have become prevalent in Canada. In 2002 senior officers profess a commitment to it, and mission statements, agency documents, and websites "talk the talk" of community policing. But what exactly community policing is operationally, how to get there, and what the measurable goals would be, especially without de-stabilising or disassembling the traditional structure of police organisations, is less convincingly evident in Canada. Acceptance by the rank-and-file and by police associations also appears wanting.

Research in Canada and in the United States suggests that police officers, including their unions, do not really understand or accept community policing. Not only do they fail to support the concept and practices, they may oppose it (Kratcoski and Dukes, 1995:140; Morris, 1997:99). The traditional commitment to reactive duties, and shift structures and organisational models built about such duties, are familiar and institutionalised, including in union contracts.

Also, the 1990s witnessed organisational changes by way of the merger of police services in Canada, rural, suburban, and urban; these large bodies have impeded and even contradicted community-based decentralisation. Finally, most recently, and possibly of major import, the passive and active resistance to reform under the banner of community policing may now be threatened by a nervous and security-conscious public — and governments — embracing enhanced and more centralised police powers in the context of a fear of terrorism. Possibly, just as Peel's original conception of policing slipped away, so too its re-invention in modern community policing may fail thorough implementation.

Three

Community Policing Template

Dennis Forcese

Introduction

The commentary that follows attempts to itemise the components of comprehensive community policing. The inventory is meant to suggest a community policing system as contrasted with piece-meal amendments that are usually presented as community policing. The chapter assumes that community-based systems, as opposed to community-based components, are by and large not in place in Canada. Also in this chapter, as a fundamental practical consideration, given the unionised environment of policing in Canada, police associations are given particular attention. Their collective agreements represent the contractual parameters for the changed work of police officers expected in a community policing system. In the final analysis, however, the itemisation that follows is but words; what is really needed is an empirically based best-practices inventory.

Ambiguities of Community Policing

Community policing is, for now, the ascendant concept in Canadian policing, at least as a label for police managers and government bureaucrats. Related and complementary concepts had been part of the Canadian policing vocabulary for many years: team policing, zone policing, village policing, store-front policing, problem-oriented policing. All have had currency, but now have been subsumed under the rubric of community policing. So widespread and untroublesome has the apparent policy commitment been to something called community policing that there is concern that community policing, like the flavour of the month, is simply the latest descriptive fad to suggest reform in the absence of fundamental change.

Police: Selected Issues

Commonly, for example, one encounters "new-think" expositions of community policing, especially as represented by consultants who seek to impress those who care to listen — perhaps those already converted — that community policing is revolutionary. For example, there is the familiar notion that community policing represents a "paradigm-shift," a change in the fundamental conception, vision, priorities, structure, and processes of policing (Gandz, 1990; Huey, 1991). And those with the will and the wit to engage the process are "paradigm shifters" and have the "paradigm advantage."

Such "hype-speak" suggests that the notion may have been over-sold by academics and professional "change-agents". Moreover, as perhaps part of the over-sell, where operational prototypes are in place, too much success is then attributed to some version of so-called community policing. One might cite a recent American example and speculate that New York City Police Department (NYPD) community policing might account for successive years of reduced crime. Or there are claims, for which at least there are some supportive research findings, that community policing will reinvigorate the working experiences of police officers. For example, the organisational shift to community policing in the city of Halifax, Nova Scotia in the late 1980s was sold in the familiar philosophical or theoretical context of "quality of working life" (QWL) for police personnel as well as improved relations with the public (Clairmont, 1990:18–21).

The ambiguities of the concept have not gone un-noticed. Even advocates will acknowledge that the concept is vague, shifty, all-encompassing, even "elusive" (Friedmann, 1992:2–3), and means different things to different people — perhaps more importantly, it means what area police services say they are doing. Also a class bias is remarked, as police "community" collaboration is effected with relatively stable and conforming middle-class populations, and not with the urban segments historically associated with intensive police activity. The ambiguities are not likely to convert traditionalists in policing who doubt the efficacy of "wishy-washy" consultations with "squeaky-wheel" community representatives and of ill-defined and unmeasured expectations and outcomes in lieu of good old-fashioned clearance rates. Additionally "old" police managers ponder the realities, as have academics, of entrenched police personnel, practices, and interests, and fail to find the necessary motivation or skills to approximate the proactive concepts suggested by community policing. Perhaps more fundamentally, beyond the traditional scepticism, those "new" police managers intent upon somehow realising the mandated community-based policing, find themselves asking — even demanding — to be told precisely what is meant, and what is necessary to achieve it, especially in the context of collective agreements, shift schedules, and budgetary stress.

The Canadian Association of Chiefs of Police, responding to some member perplexity, has tentatively sought to commission work to document and to specify operationally the definitions and experiences of community policing and associated management and organisational changes. Similarly, the Solicitor General of Ontario, having embedded the concept in Ontario's statutes, year after year attempts to develop "how-to-do" handbooks, just as "how-to-do" textbooks have found their way onto the American market (eg., Miller and Hess, 1994). The Ontario Provincial Police offer a do-it-yourself manual for community policing implementation. In both Canada and the United States, such directions have tended to consist of lists of community policing components rather more than operational guides to implement those components applicable by managers contending with resistant employees. To the extent that directions for practice are provided, they focus upon the nature of relations with community groups and also, in some measure, discussion of the skills and related training that would be required by police personnel for this "new" mode of policing. In the matter of training, even as police colleges have moved to community policing modules, the instructional content, as historically may be said of recruit training, is subsequently overwhelmed by the realities of police work when, as police say, the real education begins.

In general, therefore, the vaunted shift to community policing has lacked a precision of operational definition and of empirical examples. Accordingly, there is considerable variation in the extent to which the concept is grasped, attempted, and evaluated in Canadian police services (Kennedy, 1991:280–282), which is also true of the United States (Moore, 1992:127–139). As already mentioned, Canadian police services do attempt measures that are presented as community policing. There do appear to be sincere, broadly based prototypes that conform to the features generally suggested in the literature as intrinsic to community policing. These prototypes, however, are not well-evaluated, and moreover, even as some competent evaluations have been conducted, the results have been equivocal at best. Moreover the evaluation results appear rather be directed more to the attention of academics and some policymakers rather than to police managers or even to po-

lice service boards. Formal evaluations of major community policing initiatives have not translated into best practices information
or instructions that are exportable to other police services (Clairmont, 1990; Walker and Walker, 1989; Walker et al., 1992; Hornick,
Burrows, Tjosvold, and Phillips, 1990; Hornick, Burrows, Phillips,
and Leighton, 1991; Hornick, Leighton, and Burrows, 1993), although at least in one instance, an evaluation appeared to inform
the continued efforts of the Edmonton Police Service (Hornick,
Leighton, and Burrows, 1993).

Thus, even as community policing is embraced as the modern conception of policing, and has come to be the "buzz" concept
in many police organisations wishing to convey an image of progressive policing, it is less than clear what changes need actually
occur, or what measurable benefits might follow. The rhetoric or
language of policing has adapted somewhat, and some have argued that "rhetoric and practices are entwined" (Greene and Mastrofski, 1988; Ericson et al., 1993:37) and that the rhetoric of leaders can itself be a tool of organisational agenda-setting and change
(Moore, 1992:105). But it is not convincingly the case that there
has been a real paradigm-shift, that is, a change in the fundamental definition of the way things are done, let alone demonstrable structural change. The concept is often not well articulated
and the alterations that occur in the structure of the police organisations and services are often marginal and "apart from the
mainstream" (Clairmont, 1990:2) of the well-entrenched organisational structure. The separable components of community policing may be introduced piecemeal, with discernable benefit, but
fail to achieve an integrated and complementary system or structure that fundamentally amends the relations of the police to its
public (Ontario, 1994:5-6).

A Community Policing Checklist

Because a best-practises template is not available, and because
community policing rhetoric and public commitments have tended
to run ahead of practical information, community policing in
Canada has tended to marginal add-ons to the otherwise una-
mended traditional police organisation. Not only is there no "instruction kit" but also there is rarely a budget, and innovations in
the name of community policing are often left to donor funding.
In contemplating a "template," therefore, it may be stated here as
a base premise that *appropriate funding* should be entrenched in
the budget, and not be expected to be found by means of finessing

the established budget or by public appeals to merchants.

Co-incident with developing a real budget, an operational definition of community policing depends upon an informed *definition of community areas*. These may not be consonant with existing political boundaries or with historical conceptions of the community composition because of demographic shifts. In delivering community policing, information, community intelligence, or "environmental scanning" are elemental; so too in the set-up phase, in defining communities, the quality of information regarding proto-communities is basic to the designation of areas and the appropriate police services plan. Access to established public data files, or more usually polling and surveys, are needed. Presently, for example, such specialised capacity for community surveys has been established for the Ontario Provincial Police.

Community profiles need to be developed (Ontario, 1994) and the correct identification of community leaders and influential people for purposes of co-planning and service consultation is itself a critical matter for careful contemplation and action. Infrequently, however, does there appear to have been such systematic research and analysis in Canadian community policing start-ups. The intuitive police knowledge of communities is instead pragmatically, impatiently, and economically adapted to some highly profiled initiative. The community partners often are arbitrarily or superficially designated on the basis of a "squeaky-wheel" local prominence or prior relations with the police service. The general public seems usually to be blissfully — or not so blissfully — unaware of a change in policing style.

In committing to community designations, sheer size must be weighed as a factor. The size of a jurisdiction and the perceived sub-communities, the extent of differentiation economically, ethnically, and by age, and the nature of political and non-political local organisation, will impact upon any police attempts to deliver community policing. For example, for the Halifax Police Department, the city of Halifax was defined to consist of three "zones," and inevitably, therefore, there is a high degree of differentiation or heterogeneity within the "communities" that affects the ability of police to coordinate effectively with residents and results in an inevitable diminishment of the presumed affirmative impacts of community policing strategies and practices. In the city of Victoria, five areas or "communities" were broken out. In each of these instances — Halifax and Victoria — one area incorporated the city core of transient residents, commuters, businesses, and entertainment sites — that is, an area not generally constituting "community" as the concept is usually understood, and probably not as amenable as more stable residential areas to the techniques of community-based policing. Community policing cannot transform the management of problems in high intensity urban core areas with a high proportion of transients or persons in no sense residents or members of a local community (Walker et al., 1992:97).

Such urban areas are distinguishable and call for distinguishable police responses. In general, let us flag the point that community policing must allow for *variance or customisation in police services*, as all community areas are not created identical. In urban core areas not only might there be unique police responses and programs, a practice fully intended in the decentralised community policing model, there probably need also be distinct evaluative measures.

Given reasonably designated communities, the outcomes touted as being associated with community policing (improved public satisfaction and confidence, improved allocation of resources in a manner consonant with public needs and expectations, improved crime prevention and enforcement) are conceded to depend upon *coordinated public agency responses* to the social problems of an urbanised, mobile, heterogeneous population. "*Partnerships*" have become the most familiar word in the vocabulary of community policing advocates. These partnerships, however, have not arisen from the grassroots but have been assigned by policy-makers for development by the police. Curiously, the Canadian police appear to have been challenged by government policy makers as a consequence of police-initiated arguments that they are at the limits of conventional enforcement and prevention. Having propagated this view the police have found themselves obliged to assume a leadership role in the invention of new community-based partnerships. Cited approvingly and encouragingly to Canadian police managers, for example, is the ethic and the model of the Netherlands, where a National Police Coordination Centre representing Dutch police services has stressed the front-line role of police in acting with government and other agencies in crime prevention (Horn, 1991:129). Another pre-condition of implementation, therefore, is a sustained *information campaign for public awareness and interest*. Such a campaign depends upon a different kind of partnership, one with opinion leaders in the community, such as media representatives, academics, religious leaders, and ethnic association leaders. In so doing, the police spokespersons must be committed to the task for the long-term, rather than have the community experience a constant succession of community officers.

It is generally agreed that the necessary components of community policing include *stable police assignment* in the definable geographic territory or community; a focus upon community relations in the sense of interactive communications, consultation, and cooperation; an emphasis upon crime prevention and proactive policing; a decentralisation of police organisational authority and the traditional bureaucratic hierarchy; fewer role specialisations; and, a greater reliance upon the front-line police officer as generalist, whose tasks include criminal investigation (Wasson, 1975:22-25; Ontario, 1994; Kennedy, 1991; Forcese, 1999: 118-122, 286-287).

The community policing expectation of stable assignment of police personnel mirrors the intent to know and to work with local area residents. That is, the police officers in an area are expected to become familiar with a zone and its inhabitants, and vice versa. The police themselves are not to be transient. It is also desirable to have stable and readily identifiable police offices or buildings in the local area, rather than minor ancillary facilities, characteristically ad hoc and often uninviting, especially in the start-up phase of decentralised community policing.

Moreover, in this stable capacity, the police are, in the model, expected to have *decentralised responsibility* for the area once community-based police services are initiated. That is, the highly specialised and centralised police organisations are to be altered by way of more local authority and responsibility, including investigatory, vested in the police constable or patrol officer. Additionally in the community area, the officers are expected to work within a cooperative local team definition or structure.

Organisational problems arise not only for traditional management but also for traditional police job expectations, including, perhaps above all, for detectives and criminal investigations units. The above characteristics — decentralised control and the generalist role — are intended to enhance communications and the quality of contact and work with members of the public: a re-invention of the somewhat mythological precinct system of policing just as there is also a re-invention of the somewhat mythological community. Parenthetically it may be remarked that there is some less than unanimous opinion that to effect quality community contacts, the community area officers must, in greater frequency, be on foot rather than being committed to vehicular patrol (Greene and Taylor, 1988).

Police: Selected Issues

Community policing depends upon enhanced *police–public communications* and other contacts. The implication generally understood is of police personnel in more frequent benign and consultative communications with members of a "community." The contacts are to be at all levels, with front-line personnel and not just command-rank personnel now engaging members of the community, and interacting with people other than elected political representatives, offenders, or victims (Roach, 1986:86). This engagement or communication may occur not only in the street but also in the committee and board rooms of corporate and civic organisations within the communities — a matter of some concern to critical police-watchers. Related to enhanced communications, preventive policing will involve greater police participation in municipal policy-making and the activities of other public services. Examples include participation with educators or with urban and social planners (see Lunney, 1989:204–205). Police participation in youth education and immigrant education, in building design, and in client referrals to support agencies would all be expected to become frequent and normative. Thoroughgoing police engagement in the policy formulation and services of the community is intended to meet the basic community policing expectation of more preventive policing, and general assistance to the public, as distinct from law enforcement and criminal investigation. Yet in Canada in particular this is a point of tension in that the police distance from political action has been historically much more pronounced than in the United States.

The police–public contacts and communications are expected to be two-way or interactive, wherein public views influence the police service as contrasted with a situation where segments of the public are passive recipients of police-derived information. There is reason to state that this is one of the most difficult conditions to meet. Even as patrol-level contacts and speaking engagements may increase, there is a tendency for the public to defer to the police as "experts." Also, the police organisation may not have in place the resources and skills to collect, collate, analyse, and disseminate information available from public participation (Seagrave, 1992; Tremblay and Rochon, 1991). A deliberate program of environmental scanning, with analysis of available information such as that from local media, and the generation of additional representative information through means such as information surveys or polls, appear requisites to enhance other routine information gathering.

Returning to the idea of paradigm-shift and the rhetoric or

language of community policing, as the policing task becomes more service- and client-oriented, some of the terminology of traditional para-military policing, in reference to the public and perhaps in regard to internal organisation designations of ranks, or of the community zones or areas themselves, becomes "civilianised" and connote the objective that has been called "total quality service." To illustrate, perhaps trivially: one American police force deleted from its motto the conventional reference "to protect" in order to highlight "to serve" (Galloway and Fitzgerald, 1992:5)! Or, to illustrate the absence of such a language shift, in Halifax the three community policing zones are encumbered with the para-military labels Alpha, Bravo, and Charlie zones, failing to symbolise for the public any community identification through labelling.

Given all of the above, the essence of the change to community policing is the downloading of tasks and responsibilities to the front-line police officers who are associated with the designated communities. Consider the conventionally agreed police functions of response, enforcement, crime solving, prevention, referral, and public education. Where, in the traditional policing mode, only the first two of these functions will be associated with the traditional front-line patrol officer, in community policing all six functions are part of the job (Clairmont, 1990:42). In particular, the community police officer becomes more than a reactive "complaints-taker." For decades there has been speculation, largely wishful, about the police officer as "professional," whereas in traditional policing, the officer, and especially the patrol officer has been rather more like a piece-worker than a professional, doing very limited and segmented work. Community policing, however, does genuinely allow for, and require, the front-line police officer as a professional.

Within this general concept or model there is room for variation. Budget imperatives will, of course, impact upon implementation, as will training requirements. The initial decentralisation, for example, may therefore not be total or jurisdiction-wide, although there is some reason to argue for wholesale introduction, but instead be phased in for one or a few community areas. The areas may be large and few, or many and small. The generalist role may be intrinsic and thoroughgoing from the outset, or dedicated initially to specified target areas or storefront or "village" operations.

If economic and personnel considerations oblige a gradualist approach to jurisdiction-wide community policing, it is imperative that the staging occur within the context of a full implementation plan, with clearly defined operational objectives, including target dates. Piecemeal community-policing with no explicit commitment to system-wide change will tend to be cosmetic and will inevitably produce damaging distinctions among personnel and publics (Walker and Walker, 1989; Clairmont, 1990; Walker et al., 1992).

The transformation in policing that is effected by the above measures is, of course, intended to be more than cosmetic. There are to be demonstrable consequences. Three key outcome areas should be noted. In the first instance, public satisfaction with policing may be expected to improve, including public perceptions of safety (Kennedy, 1991:282-287; Peak et al., 1992; Walker et al., 1992:67-70). The cooperative and consultative relations with residents, including targetted sub-groups such as seniors, should favourably influence perceptions.

The preventive orientation of community policing, along with the consultative relations and inter-agency cooperation, may be expected to influence crime rates and solutions (Walker and Walker, 1989:10-23). However, any shift in reported offenses and clearances poses a somewhat complicated problem insofar as being an indicator of community policing success. Generalist constable investigators, for example, especially in the earlier phases of a community-based system, may suffer from lack of training, inexperience, and problems in overall workload management, in turn potentially adversely affecting public confidence and willingness to report offences. Alternatively, reported offences may increase rather than decrease, in that the closer contacts of community policing and increased public confidence may be expected to encourage greater public willingness to report violations (Clairmont, 1990; Kennedy, 1991:282-283). As well, offence rates may increase as a reflection of the "expanded police mandate" (Koenig, 1991:35) that is a feature of contemporary policing and particularly associated with community policing. Clearance by charges, or otherwise, will also be affected by referral options, and by enhanced information vested in closer community contacts; the emergent measurable trend-line is not easily predictable.

From the experience of other police services, we can, of course, anticipate some of the consequences for police employees. On the basis of information gleaned from Canadian reports on Victoria and Halifax (Walker and Walker, 1989:66-77; Clairmont, 1990:4-6, 141-148; Walker et al., 1992:28-30) or from the American assessment of Reno, Nevada (Peak et al., 1992), it is possible to anticipate outcomes elsewhere, both the positive and the potentially negative and contentious.

Community policing may be expected — and has been shown to — result in increased police job satisfaction (Clairmont, 1990; Walker et al., 1992). The decentralisation and broadening of responsibilities associated with community policing constitute a "skilling" of the front-line police officer, and an extension to them of professional responsibilities. Not only do public perceptions of policing alter in a community policing environment, so too do the perceptions of police employees.

One relatively clear outcome is increased job satisfaction by most employees, especially police constables, as greater task responsibilities are provided. Probably indicative of increased satisfaction has been a finding of reduced sick leave days. Yet, in fairness it must also be noted that there is some indication that the greater emphasis upon pro-active and generalist work, while appreciated by most, and especially by "beat" or foot officers in more frequent public contact, if not reinforced with an effective system of evaluation and recognition, may be found to be insufficiently exciting or rewarding. Disproportionately, people in some ranks, such as inspectors, may find themselves functionally displaced as responsibilities are downloaded. The redistribution of detective functions, with the probable exception of "major crimes," is characteristically noted in the research/evaluation literature.

Dependent upon pre-implementation training, some basic functions such as the investigatory, may, as distributed, be perceived to suffer. Job assignment and responsibility on the basis of seniority is, of course, all but eliminated and the seniority system therefore weakened, to the satisfaction of many and the dissatisfaction of some. New demands for coordination and communication occur, taken up at least temporarily by a flurry of meetings, memoranda, guidelines, and reports. Workloads may increase, or be perceived to increase, as new tasks are assumed by front-line personnel. It is not unusual to find demand for additional personnel, and there is evidence of some increase in civilian employees in support roles. In addition there is experience of some increase in the number of non-commissioned officers, and a comparable decrease in commissioned officers, as local co-ordinating needs are associated with the decentralised duties assigned to front-line officers (Clairmont, 1990:76–78).

Employee Group Cooperation

Rather than being merely sceptical the police rank and file and their associations are often opposed to measures associated with community policing. They tend to consider community policing to be a threat to genuine police work, and in contemplating a demand for different skills, work styles, hours, training, and education, a threat to their careers. The implications of collective agreements, as they relate, for example, to promotions, shift schedules, and overtime, are the practical considerations that a chief of police must navigate in attempting to reconfigure a police service for the delivery of thoroughgoing community policing. It is the nature of community policing to require a group participatory dynamic in its implementation and continuation. Right from the outset, therefore, implementation depends upon a *consultative and collaborative process* (Wilgus, 1991) that perhaps has not been very prevalent in Ontario police services, and that might be characterised by some as co-opting and by others as co-management. Any negative loading of such words must simply be over-ridden, in the realisation that all parties to the change process are adapting and that ultimately the community policing objective is a redefinition of roles that fundamentally re-distributes decision-making and authority.

Following from the initial step of *joint employee-management commitment* to community-based policing, the joint preparation, refinement, and conveyance to all employees of an implementation program must be achieved. Thus, association/management/board consultative and problem-solving bodies become a continuing element in the implementation of community policing. Depending upon the political environment, it may be advisable also to involve local political representatives and, certainly, some number of influential community members as public representatives. In the jargon of the organisational literature, there is a need for "participative leadership," with that leadership or steering assumed at the outset by management and employee association representatives who are empowered to act (Gandz, 1990; Janson and Gunderson, 1990/91; Marson, 1991). An implementation overview, or planning or steering co-committee is an imperative, as are ancillary joint groups or steering teams to implement specifics in the redesign and reassignment of the work or roles in the police service (Wilgus, 1991).

There probably also needs to be an explicit decision that the overview committee be empowered to make binding and consensual recommendations for implementation. One key recommendation that might best emanate from such a committee would be one calling for no start-up changes in the collective agreement and, related to this, the recommendation that complaints and grievances associated with altered work assignment deriving from community policing be suspended or carried over for a start-up or trial period of probably at least one year's duration. Thereafter, work to amend the language and provisions of an agreement may receive some priority attention, including attention to preamble language that invokes a commitment to the concept of community policing and thereby enshrines the changed philosophy or paradigm.

Additionally, before and throughout the trial period, joint work on training programs, job descriptions, and evaluation criteria must occur. Reflexive training, that is, training in response to evolving information and working conditions, is a necessity, as the very concepts that serving members have of their jobs are being altered (van Maanen and Katz, 1979). Not the least important aspect of retraining will have to do with old skills, such as in investigations, as much as with the newer skills associated with interpersonal communications in a pro-active community policing culture. There is no pretending that traditional reactive functions will disappear, but priorities and responses will alter as will the participants.

Associated with the amended job roles will be the need for job descriptions, new evaluation and promotions measures, and possibly a new rank structure. Role and performance uncertainties are to be expected and must be resolved. While there are research data to suggest that there is greater job satisfaction for police officers in a work environment where they have fuller responsibilities and autonomy, there is no avoiding the fact that the increased satisfaction will also vary with factors such as age, time in career, and in some measure, by rank and present job function. As some number of specialised roles are eliminated, new career opportunities — and frankly, new prestige opportunities — have to be made available, and may eventually be referenced in collective agreements.

Collaborative design and implementation throughout is the effective and constructive way to begin the implementation of a system of policing that, in its fundamental definition, extends more job responsibility and more job complexity to more police officers. Deliberately and stubbornly, familiar views of command, rank and deference, and of adversarial problem-solving must be put aside. Over the long term, if community policing "takes" as a genuine fundamental organisational change, the style of employee relations that will come to be prevalent or part of the culture of the organisation will be more collegial. Such collegial, professional, and team-task achievement will not obviate the need for employee groups and collective agreements: unions, grievances, and job actions do occur in professional/collegial organisations, as in universities, for example. But there should be some displacement of the formal adversarial style that often comes to be institutionalised in employee-management relations. Transition to a co-problem solving style or ethic, informally and at times formally, perhaps resorting to such mechanisms as conflict mediation, will be encouraged by the cooperative implementation of community policing. The joint committee structure for policy and action, and the community-based committees linking with the public, will come to deal with issues that might otherwise accumulate for the bargaining table or confound effective delivery of services. Bargaining issues will increasingly be formulated in the context of awareness of community needs and the needs of police officers in generating good and effective relations with community residents. The community, in effect, will be consulted. Ideally, too, the cooperative mode would lead to employee participation, that is, police association employee membership and participation, on police services boards in a manner comparable to union/association membership on university boards of governors. In general, therefore, even as there is no reason to require or to expect that collective bargaining will be incompatible with community policing, the very nature of decentralised community policing may moderate the adversarial quality that often characterises the collective bargaining process.

These considerations before us, there remain questions as to police contracts. In the typical collective agreement where are there obstacles to the implementation of community policing? Or, alternatively, what features should be avoided or suspended in collective agreements if there is to be a good-faith attempt to shift a complex police organisation to community-based policing services? Given the objective of a transformation of a police service, that is, jurisdiction-wide community areas with decentralised or relatively autonomous discretion for area personnel, what changes might be required of employee-management relations for effective implementation? The following observations are made on the basis of a review of Ontario police collective agreements.

Perhaps previous observations make evident that much of the change associated with community-based policing is not explicitly referenced in collective agreements, except perhaps as one might wish to resort to the ubiquitous "past practice." Yet the transformations described do impact upon contract specifications. To do community policing, then, what contract changes may be required?

One could actually respond: none. At least, let us suggest, none in the first instance. Having perused several collective agreements in Ontario, and discussed the implications of community-based policing with police officers in Ontario and elsewhere, it appears that there is sufficient scope within the agreements now in place to implement community-based policing, if the parties are generally agreed to such an attempt. If they are not agreed, changes are unlikely to be achieved at any rate, and opposition, including formal grievances and job action, would obstruct effective implementation.

A major intent of this response is to stress that the successful introduction of community policing depends upon a shared start-up interest, if not commitment, and upon flexibility. Rather than attempt to anticipate and perhaps inadvertently build in impediments, existing agreements should be flexibly maintained, and only eventually might negotiated changes follow from evaluated implementation of altered community-based policing services.

In effect, at the outset the process might be to suspend contract language provisions that impede measures that all parties agree are necessary to the introduction and operation of community policing. The police association, police management, the police services board, and in its avuncular way, the provincial government, must understand and agree that any dissatisfactions and grievances arising from changed roles in the move to a community policing environment are to be held over for post-implementation analysis and resolution. Similarly, any changes in collective agreements should occur after a period of planned implementation and evaluation, on the basis of experience and subsequently identified need, if any, of contract amendments.

There appear to be at least six closely related key elements appropriately included, referenced in, or directly related to collective agreements that might have a bearing upon the conceptual and operational character of community policing.

Job definitions, even as currently not usually referenced explicitly in collective agreements and only defined by past practice, must in some measure be stipulated. Most positions in community policing will stress the generalist police role, and these professional duties should be captured in more formal job descriptions and/or some parameter-setting contract language in order to assist the employee and in order concurrently to move to an appropriate personnel evaluation/reward system. In community policing, for most people the job will change not only at implementation but also thereafter. The descriptions will therefore have to be flexible, mirroring the generalist duties and the community-reflexive character of the police services, and be reviewed and adjusted at regular intervals.

Some specialised jobs will exist in the decentralised community policing system, for sworn and for civilian personnel. These too will benefit from job descriptions. Examples might include training personnel, computer systems personnel, audit and information management/analysis personnel, and arguably, even redefined community crime prevention and investigatory specialists and "supervisors."

The latter deserves comment lest it be viewed as a simple contradiction of the generalist conception. In professional organisations that stress the similar skills and duties of employees, such as at a university, there are nonetheless distinguishable degrees of expertise, in part associated with inclination, and in part with streaming for efficient and comprehensive attention to diverse and complex information and service delivery. It is additionally worth remarking that in professional organisations there are persisting coordinating, supervisory and management designations — some degree of hierarchy — even as generalist responsibilities are stressed. In the decentralised police organisation, roles and the nature of supervision/management will alter by way of greater emphasis upon generalist responsibility of front-line personnel, greater consultation, and a need to coordinate rather more than to supervise or direct — but as we persist in providing the organised delivery of services, and not some sort of *laissez-faire* professionalism, some distinguishable roles, responsibilities, and accountabilities will exist.

Rank structures, and their labels, may be amended. The hierarchical differentiation that has traditionally characterised police organisations, from their inception as para-military organisations, may usefully be altered to reflect the responsibilities associated with increased generalist roles, and to reflect decentralised management or task coordination. It should be considered, however, that career progress opportunities need not become fewer. In effect, in community policing's emphasis upon generalist roles, especially in large jurisdictions, there remains, as previously noted, demand for specialist support roles. Additionally, even as there is a greater dependence upon the generalist constable, distinctions or gradations of achievement or rank will be redefined in a manner more like that of other professional organisations rather than as in the traditional para-military or bureaucratic fashion. To take an example from the educational sector, the university — where it may be fairly observed that the formal duties of an Assistant Professor and of a Full Professor are much the same — there are nonetheless distinctions of prestige, rank or status, and compensation. Presumably, these in turn are reflections of factors such as experience, expertise, competence, workload and productivity, client response, and reputation, as would be the case in community policing services.

Evaluations as related to annual review and to promotion will have to be altered as a matter of priority to incorporate criteria related to the more pro-active or prevention-oriented style of policing in the community-based system. Collective agreements tend to be silent on details of evaluation criteria, but agreements do allude to established practice, and might benefit from explicit incorporation in contract language. Communications skills, for example, will probably need to be weighted significantly. Even as there will be continuing resort to some of the traditional indicators of performance, establishing new evaluation criteria and methods consistent with the community-based standards of performance will probably be the most daunting of the tasks.

Altered performance expectations and measures may be expected to be associated with some change in the evaluators. Where it has been characteristic of large organisations and of professionals to be self-reliant or closed in performance assessment, it is increasingly evident that the demands for accountability, whether in regard to physicians, academics, teachers, or police officers, are ever more associated with some requirement of external representation in the process of performance assessment, not just in regard to alleged misconduct, but more generally. Additionally, it is evident that in addition to external participation in the process, there is some expectation that the process and the outcomes be replicable and "transparent," and therefore seen to be valid and reliable representations of community and organisational needs and standards.

Training, with emphasis upon in-service training, will have to be amended and expanded, especially in the period of transition to the new style of policing. In fact, all personnel should have to pass through a start-up orientation training program. Content emphasis will range from communications skills (for example, in the Halifax Police Department, personnel received "toastmaster" instruction), to time-management training, and investigative training for the greater responsibilities to be assigned to the community patrol officers. Mandatory in-service training is typically not spelled out in a collective agreement, even as most services will have operated programs of in-service training. Some agreement with respect to the frequency, duration, content, expectations, and costs of re-training and career-long upgrading will be necessary. This is probably a critical area for province-wide collaboration.

While there will undoubtedly be comprehensive start-up training for all personnel to some agreed schedule, it should be acknowledged that the nature of the policing style that is being attempted is one that can aptly be characterised as "reflexive." That is, there is, ideally, in community-based policing, an individual and an organisational capacity to adapt to changed circumstances and information. One could again invoke the imprecise notion of the professional person, whereby there is an expectation and a responsibility for on-going education or retraining. The community policing service will therefore have to provide for, encourage, and reward both in-house and public training access for its members. Career mobility and perhaps even career continuation will be dependent upon such ongoing education, and probably therefore, demand for access will have to be regulated; that is, a system of selection among applicants will have to be developed and agreed upon by the parties.

Compensation adjustments will become necessary, as related to agreement provisions to do with rank, "acting" pay, and with overtime. The first relates to the matter of job definitions, and the last to the requests of community members for services (for example, school visits or lectures to community associations) that do not coincide with shift schedules. In the matter of compensation and rank, as previously observed, gradations, albeit redefined, will still exist and will be reincorporated into collective agreements. Also, as in any modern organisation, compensation variations will continue to be associated with duration of employment. Rank gradations and the weight attached to seniority, however, will tend to be moderated in community policing, and in order to implement meaningful steps along the pay scale, there may be increased attention to education/training credentials and to performance evaluation as compensation criteria.

Patrol shifts will, in many instances, have to be redefined. Present language should not present an insoluble difficulty, given that there is acceptance of the first condition: flexibility. Some provisions might have to be suspended. The particular durations of shifts now conventionally in place in Ontario police services all appear adaptable to a community-based policing format. It is not evident that there are more or fewer difficulties associated with 8- or 10- or 12-hour shifts, although there is no definitive data. It may be hypothesised, for example, that shorter shift durations are more appropriate to community-based policing in order to avert extended off-duty periods that disrupt contacts and visibility in the community. Alternatively, extended shifts may be better suited to the multi-dimensional duties of the generalist constable.

Strict requirements for the number of people on patrol, or the number of patrol units in a zone or area in a given time period or shift, will be dysfunctional and will require alteration. The two-person patrol requirement, for example, while arguably appropriate to a reactive law enforcement emphasis, is probably not pertinent to most of the preventive activities that the patrol personnel in an area would be expected to take up. Similarly, available personnel will have to be available in a manner consonant with public requirement for services.

There must be flexibility of personnel assignment in response to community service needs, with determination made on a decentralised basis. The police constables as local area professionals should be accorded the opportunities to adapt to local conditions. And the local conditions will vary across community areas.

Fundamentally, collective agreements exists to define and to govern compensation, benefits, and critical conditions of work. In community policing additional emphasis may be upon language that addresses working conditions and ensures the provision of the training, infrastructure, and interpersonal support necessary for police officers to perform as competent professionals.

In general, it appears obvious that the larger the police organisation, the greater the transitional difficulties associated with the decentralising shift to community policing. Communities will have to be functionally defined, the hierarchical management command structure will have to be amended, and longstanding skills, specialisations, and ranks modified. These amendments carry the potential of contentious changes in the reward and mobility expectations of serving police personnel. Care needs be taken to prepare and to accommodate serving officers whose expectations of role and career prospects in the organisation are perceived to be disrupted and in jeopardy. No less a need is to track the changing composition, attitudes, and needs of local publics.

Summary and Conclusions

To summarise, the general start-up operational assumptions and observations can be aggregated into three considerations that stress interpersonal style and information.

First, planning and on-going implementation must be collaborative, as between the police services board, management, and employee association(s), and as between the police service and representative community sectors. The chief of police, the chairperson of the police services board, and the president of the police association all must be seen to be associated with the commitment to and the process of coordinated change. The notion of "participative leadership" is an apt summary label for the co-conduct of start-up. While there is a danger that the process be seen simply as "top–down," the major executive commitment is necessary for the subsequent participatory process to be properly engaged. Potential scare-concepts, such as co-optation, or for some, co-management, must be disregarded.

External to the organisation, at risk of creating expectations that are too great, publicity is probably desirable in order to achieve community awareness and support (Walker and Walker, 1989:57–58). Alternatively, of course, without public engagement the impact upon public perceptions, participation, and the gamut of public cooperative responses, including crime reporting, may not meet expectations.

In regard to the role of the members of the community, non-conventional participants are integral. This, in fact, may pose considerable difficulty for a police service, as public spokespersons may not be apparent and there may be a tendency for conventional political representatives to appropriate the participative opportunities. Ultimately, in achieving broadly based consultative opportunities with community residents, an objective in addition to enhanced information for purposes of both reactive and pro-active policing is a shift in perceptions, most particularly, a diminution of the fears and concerns of members of the community.

Internally, then, there is an imposition of collegial work relations in place of encapsulated bureaucratic/hierarchical work relations. Externally, there is resort to members of the public as a resource and as clients.

Second, in a collaborative or participatory leadership process, the resources of numerous people inside and outside of the organisation should be utilised, for the intended outcome is an institutionalised system of inter-dependency. At least at the outset of operations these communications will depend largely upon an abundance — probably an over-abundance — of meetings. Frequent and regular meetings among command-rank personnel, generally prevalent in most police organisations, will be supplemented by many additional configurations for purposes of coordination, policy-testing, and reaffirmation. Meetings of commissioned officers and area supervisors or representatives, meetings of community area personnel, command-rank, and area personnel with community members, including elected municipal officials, will proliferate.

In the course of these activities, rank distinctions, or more precisely, rank protocols, will have to be moderated, if not eliminated, in order to facilitate informal contact and communications.

Third, lateral and vertical communications within the police service organisation must be optimised, as contact and communications channels are similarly being established and enhanced with the members of the community. In the traditional police structure the bureaucratic hierarchy may inhibit information flow, at least, vertical flow. In community policing, the decentralised and rather autonomous responsibilities of police officers may inhibit vertical and lateral information flow, and consequent service effectiveness and efficiency.

Information deriving from communications must be systematically gathered, collated, analysed, and disseminated in order to inform the service delivery of the organisation. A research and analysis capacity, for purposes of operations and evaluation, will be necessary (Seagrave, 1992), although the capacity need not be fully internal to an individual police organisation. An explicit objective of community policing is to "increase ... intelligence information" (Walker et al., 1992:10). However, there is reason to assert that characteristically one of the greatest failings of police organisations is poor distribution of information and under-analysis of available information (Tremblay and Rochon, 1991).

A community-based system must be reflexive, responsive, and flexible. Community perceptions and demands must be identified and appraised, and performance of police service personnel must be appraised and, as necessary, amended. Put otherwise, feedback must be constructively utilised. These considerations underline the value of co-planning, and of implementation evaluation and benchmarks in order to monitor and to evaluate the changes and their consequences for police employees and for the public. Such co-participation and total community engagement will then achieve a genuinely transformed policing consonant with changed social circumstances, and perhaps become sufficiently open, sensitive, and adaptable to evolve with the continued social changes associated with the foreseeable expansion of Canada's first-generation immigrant population.

Four

Managing Information

Dennis Forcese and Nancy Lewis-Horne

Introduction

The issue considered in this chapter is that of information flow between the police and the public. Any organisation engaged in the production and delivery of goods or of services is dependent upon effective communications with its customers or clients. Private-sector organisations are especially sensitive to information-gathering for purposes of marketting and are accustomed to acquiring and conveying data. Market surveys, for example, are a well-established tool, as is advertising. For-profit corporations, too, often have to deal with crises, such as product recalls, and have invested in the means flow to information. Public-sector service organisations, such as the police, should be no less interested in information acquisition and conveyance. This is a "critical challenge" for police services seeking to develop and maintain an effective organisational culture that is responsive to the needs of the community — a service that is "customer-driven" (Adamson and Deszca, 1990:158).

The discussion that follows draws upon interviews in the early 1990s when Canadian police services were first struggling to find their way into the community policing style. Three distinguishable sectors will be considered: media relations, community relations, and public complaints. Three police organisations will be frequently remarked for illustrative purposes, and will be referred to as Service-A (S-A), Service-B (S-B), and Service-C (S-C). They were selected to provide some transitional contrast. In 1993 S-A was a substantial and viable suburban police service formally committed to community policing. S-B was a large urban police service in the early stages of contemplating community policing. S-C was also a large urban organisation but with jurisdiction-wide community policing already in place and evolving.

45

Information and Community Policing

In order to implement a commitment to community-based policing effective communications are of paramount importance. Consultation and collaboration with the community, in the interests of both law enforcement and crime prevention, are fundamental to community policing. Information must therefore be viewed as input and output, and data must be acquired from and provided to those being served and protected. Walker et al. (1992:6) have remarked that it is expected that community policing "increase the reporting of intelligence information," by which we must understand both traditional criminal or law enforcement intelligence and also preventive and service-oriented intelligence. This, of course, from a contrary view, is precisely the benefit of community policing that is criticised by some as too intrusive (Ericson and Haggerty, 1997).

Information must not only be received, it must also be organised, assessed, and applied. That is, it must be analysed and rendered functional. The usefulness of the information will relate to policy formulation and the allocation of resources and services specific to community circumstances. Information affects all levels of the organisation. Organisational information flow, therefore, must be effective, vertically and laterally, with information shared among managers and with their operatives, and there must also be information sharing among front-line personnel, operating as teams and not as individuals. Informed decisions arising from information analysis in turn should be made known to the pertinent publics or clients, and in fact, tested or re-tested in public media and meetings of community members.

Police agencies demonstrating an open or democratic model of police organisation may move closer to an ideal community-based policing implementation strategy, characterised by positive police/community relations, and effective information exchanges. Angell (1975:36) suggests that by implementing a democratic model police organisations can improve community relations, employee morale, and police operational effectiveness. From a basis of more adequate information, police services appropriate to the local community can be provided. The localised and tailored police service can rely less on the specialised and pre-packaged community program delivery services of the organisation. Instead, team members may deliver these and customised applications as part of their service delivery function, on the basis of systematically acquired and analysed broad-based social information. Environmental scanning, using techniques ranging from focus groups to polling or surveys, can be employed.

Information in Traditional Services

Traditionally police organisations have not been adept at optimising information intake or information outflow. Police agencies, closely identified with an historic para-militaristic organisational model, have had difficulty implementing interactive strategies. Sandler and Mintz (1974:459) assert that the rigid boundaries inherent in the para-military mode of traditional police organisations have created police–community distance and reinforced the isolation of the police from the community. Such a relationship mimics the authoritarian structure of the organisation, with the public being treated in a procedural, technically oriented, and legalistic manner. It can be assumed from such a description that a traditional police organisation would have difficulty promoting effective police–community information exchanges.

In traditionally structured police organisations, information out-flow has tended to be marginalised and non-systematic. It has been associated with packaged and often low-prestige community relations operations, media management, and in some sense, with the interpersonal and political contacts and interactions of the senior officers, most particularly the chief of police. By and large, information and cues are conveyed externally, to the public, in a controlled, content-sparse mode, with an emphasis upon public relations. Community relations functions in such traditional police organisations operate on the fringes of their mainstream activities. They may, for example, rely on conventional preventive pre-packages and seek community contacts by means of "storefronts" and "coffee klatches," failing to generate representative information or to reach the entire community (Cordner, 1978:34).

Similarly, as dominated by a reactive and law enforcement mode, information has been received and utilised in an improvised manner. Police services have had their information "sensing activities" associated with patrol, investigation, informants, criminal intelligence, community relations (Neave et al., 1982:133), and with complaints. There is always some information gleaned from the contacts that patrol and investigative officers have with a public, but these encounters tend to be in context of some adversarial or otherwise negative circumstance. They also tend to be incident-driven and, by and large, too, the data are the privileged information of the individual police officers who acquire the insight, benefit, and power of pertinent information. A similar characterisation relates to police utilisation of informants.

There is also community or political intelligence gained from the contacts between commissioned officers, especially the chief of police, and local area police service board members, politicians, and other notables. Such information is, of course, often skewed or biassed, tending to represent the views of persons who, despite presumed representative electoral status, may not in fact be representative of the considerable diversity that exists in most large Canadian urban jurisdictions.

Additional low-grade conventional sources of public information for police services, usually associated with the workaday habits of some commissioned officers or simply the casual press perusal of serving officers, are the media. The local press, for example, is often monitored by individual police officers, and sometimes out-of-jurisdiction media with a view to events or circumstances that may eventually come to impact locally. Few police services seem to be prepared to bear the cost of newspaper clipping services, or resort to any systematic analysis or referral of information gleaned from news reports.

Most major services, however, have operated some sort of criminal intelligence or criminal analysis operation, and, for purposes of regular reporting to the civil authority and for budget preparation, some statistical account of activity. The nearest example of police organisations attempting to systematise information is to be had in criminal intelligence operations, where data, usually information regarding offenses, are "massaged" in search of patterns or trends useful for investigative and especially for resource acquisition and allocation purposes (e.g., special task forces). Data for statistical reporting and budget arguments loom large.

But the practice of acquiring information in a proactive manner, as in environmental scanning or community research as an intelligence technique, while at times called for by police managers (Lunney, 1989:204–205), is very rare. There have been some attempts to scan the community, as in surveys conducted for police services (Horne, 1993), but even these characteristically have not been sought for operational purposes so much as for evaluative and public relations purposes.

Internally, information flow is very hierarchical, flowing down and associated with the authority structure, with scant lateral communications at any level, but perhaps especially deficient between mid-managers and between front-line personnel (Adamson,

1987:247–249). Moreover, the communications tend to be written (Adamson and Deszca, 1990:168–169). Non-commissioned personnel in particular have perceived the hierarchical and formal character of communications (Adamson, 1987:245–246) while managers have been somewhat insensitive to the impact of formal communications (Adamson and Deszca, 1990:166). Vertical information flow, therefore, has been found to be imperfect, dependent upon often complex written communiqués or orders, and non-participatory or management-dominated. While some police managers are sensitive to these features and have publicly remarked on the need for more informal and "interpersonal communication" (Lunney, 1989:199), one may generally still find rank-dominated manifestations of the para-military character of pre-community policing ideology and structure shaping the information flow (Adamson, 1987), usually simply characterised as top-down.

Three case organisations and three communications task areas are considered briefly, to further illustrate the issue.

Media Relations

Media relations within Canadian police services have tended to consist of one or a few individuals who are charged with the task of co-ordinating and controlling media releases. Each of the three police services selected here as cases had worked with a media relations officer, one individual of non-commissioned rank with elemental training by way of a Canadian Police College course in media and communications. Each of the police agencies had clear policy directives advising upon the release of information. Each service had an internally distributed written statement of policy and operational practices.

While there was in each service a designated media person, there was some disagreement among the three services as to the extent of decentralisation in media contact. In the case of S–B a senior officer stated that officers were free to speak with media representatives. This was corroborated in other interviews, suggesting that criminal investigation personnel had some discretion in regard to media statements, especially when the media relations officer was not on duty. Yet at the same time, lower-ranking members of the service indicated that they did not consider that it was prudent, or even tolerable, that they would at their own discretion convey information to a news reporter, a view confirmed by a police association representative. However, the journalist in-

49

terviewed contradicted this information somewhat, by suggesting that lower-ranking members of police organisations do provide the occasional off-the-record comments. Also, he suggested that he circumvents the "boring" prepared news releases which are faxed to local press, by contacting investigative officers directly. This reporter, incidentally, was provided space in the police building.

There was scant discretionary communication in S-A, even as there was an ostensible commitment to community-based policing. The distinct expression of decentralised media contacts was in S-C, an organisation that had been operating a jurisdiction-wide community policing system, characterised by decentralised decision-making and generalist policing. Yet, in fact, contrary to interview claims, the control over media communications was effectively vested in one individual who reported to the chief of police, through the deputy chief administration. All media contacts, with the exception of initiatives taken by the chief of police, were mediated through this media relations officer. He did, however, delegate interviews to other members of the service, and in so doing, as with his own statements, advised his administrative superiors.

Media relations officers spoke of notifying their supervisors as to the content of their releases as a courtesy. The individuals releasing information to the media were also very careful to receive prior approval from supervisors regarding major issues. Personnel interviewed spoke of the risk that media releases regarding sensitive issues could offend some community groups such as visible minority groups. Consequently, review and approval by senior officers, including the chief or deputy chief in certain instances, was normal. In each of the three services the reporting line was through the deputy chief (administration) to the chief of police, with a practice of relatively informal direct access to the chief as necessary.

The media relations officers attempted to represent policy issues, but more often they conveyed investigatory or incident-related information. For example, in S-C the media relations officer would attend all major crime scenes and appeared to have the confidence of media representatives that his information releases were knowledgeable. In S-B, however, there was some perception that the media relations officer was providing second-hand and low-grade information to the media.

In each case the criminal or law enforcement information was that which was most effectively conveyed to the media. Policy or human relations stories were more difficult, except as related, perhaps, to budget. In S–C, for example, accurate information in regard to attempted innovations associated with community policing were difficult to place in the media. In part this skewing is attributable to the traditional role specialisation within newspapers, where the police services are defined as the police reporter's beat, and the police reporter (as opposed, for example, to the lifestyles reporter) is to deal in crime news, or perhaps items related to police conduct. There was the not-surprising opinion expressed by members of the agencies that the media are interested in sensational issues — that a good story will contain the elements of sex and violence. For his part, the journalist interviewed expressed professional scepticism of police statements from S–B, especially puffery, and was anxious not to be co-opted or manipulated.

Police respondents interviewed suggested much more training, preparation, and time would be necessary in order to improve access to the media. In that regard there was periodic consideration of hiring a media relations professional, but the pervasive distrust of non-police spokespersons deterred such a measure. Interestingly, the distrust was shared by the news reporter. The journalist interviewed thought that a press office in a police headquarters building was a positive aspect of good media–police relations. However, he was very concerned about the possibility of the S–B hiring a media relations professional. He believed that this would result in the 'slow, manipulative release of news."

Ericson (1989:208) identifies the value to police agencies of reporter space in a police facility, and by implication, also the benefit to a police service of a professional media person. He argues that, just as the police are agents of social control, so are the media by virtue of their gate-keeping role in regard to information. Ericson states that the "police try to incorporate the news media as part of the policing apparatus" (1989:208). One way of doing this is to provide journalists with their own offices within the police building.

Like many police services, the three case services also did manage to regularise some newspaper content. Each of the police services arranged for regular publication of crime incidents in local weekly or daily newspapers, according to neighbourhood occurrences, itemising incidents such as mischief, residential break-and-enters, and theft of or from vehicles. They also included some brief content that was preventive or advisory in nature, such as "Tips" in regard to "Violence against the elderly" or what to do if one was a "victim of wife assault." Sometimes a full-page report was produced in an insert format, to highlight an issue. In one edition the insert, "Eye on Crime," resembled a wanted poster format, with a photograph and the caption, "Armed man sought." No preventive or service content was included in this issue of "The Police File," other than telephone numbers for reports and for "Crime Stoppers." In another issue, however, "Eye on Crime" was more preventive in content, featuring a photograph of the staff sergeant heading the break-and-enter unit, and advice regarding the tendency of thieves to steal compact discs.

Generally, media relations were seen as one-way, with police attempting to manage the information flow to the media. There did not seem to be any deliberate effort to employ media content as useful intelligence. Published news reports were of course noted, but not systematically. In none of the three police services was there resort to media clipping services nor a systematic perusal and analysis of local media reports. One police service did, however, pay for access to the on-line newspaper content service of the major city newspaper, and did call up reports as they were considered to be relevant. The absence of an analysis unit charged with the task of monitoring and evaluating news items was noteworthy in all three jurisdictions. Also absent was the idea that such a systematic function would be useful to the police organisation.

Yet, each service could offer instances in which information pertinent to a major investigation was received informally from media contacts. Instances were related, for example, where the media provided information to the police, as in the instance when an individual journalist with a close relationship to the police agency acted as an ombudsman for a victim who had not received prompt, sensitive assistance from the police organisation. More general examples included tracking of crime trends in other large urban settings, providing a possible source of predictability of crime in their community, and alerting the police agency to community concerns, such as the identification of individuals released into the community who are considered to be high-risk dangerous offenders.

Community Relations

More generic community relations were variously managed in the three services. In all three services, of course, there was still some dependence upon status-based community contacts, that is, the information gained by virtue of top-level political contacts and public events, usually involving the chief of police.

In the two services most intent upon explicit community policing in the early 1990s, rank-and-file police officers appeared more likely to participate frequently in public events, including policy- and other decision-making community groups. In the service without a community policing commitment at the time, on the other hand, S-B respondents indicated that they believed that such actions without prior command approval would be subject to discipline. While senior officers and formally designated community relations officers tended to communicate with leaders and other notables, and therefore to have information and views reflecting organised groups or sub-groups, constables tended to interact with individual members of the community, often in the context of some adversarial or otherwise negative circumstance. In the organisation, therefore, there was the possibility of divergent perspectives between front-line officers, for example, and formal community relations personnel and ranking police officers.

Discrete community relations units were still in place in two of the case services, although in one instance, S-A, the unit appeared to have a more decentralised function, associated with the dispersed suburban character of its jurisdiction and decentralised community policing. The practice of this service's unit was to retain responsibility for the delivery of packaged programs in the areas of crime prevention and education with the community services section. However, in an attempt to devolve responsibilities to the zone personnel for policing issues in their area, requests for presentations from the service to community groups was being shared between the community services section and the patrol divisions. In a second organisation, S-B, the community relations-style unit responsible for education and prevention programs had been recently decentralised to the individual districts, with reporting to district commanders. The traditional programs offered by the community relations unit remained a specialised function, with specific constables being assigned community program responsibilities.

In S-C, the organisation with the most developed community policing style, rather than a community relations unit there was massive dependence upon each of the three community relations officers (constable rank) in the three zones. The community relations officers had local discretion in delivering programs, and free-ranging access to personnel, including senior officers, within the police service.

Characteristically community relations functions in police

organisations have been marginalised from mainstream policing. In the three services under study, marginalisation of the community relations functions appeared least evident in the smaller suburban service with a policy commitment to community policing and in the larger community-based service. In the latter especially, the community officer was in a position to actively influence or use patrol officers in the zone of responsibility.

Communication with the community was pursued by the three police agencies via various techniques. Conveying "packaged" prevention programs was an element of the community relations programs in all three services, as was response to community requests for information or police participation in events. While the basic preventive and information packages were utilised in all three services, it was apparent that as the services sought to implement some manner of community policing they were more likely to resort to additional outreach and information-collection measures.

In each of the services steps had been taken to identify and contact community agencies, at least for diversionary referrals. Thus, mechanisms were in place to accomplish two-way communication with the community. The Service-A and Service-C police both had encouraged zone personnel to participate and take an active interest in the communities they policed. Constables were encouraged to identify problem areas and to consult with community members, and front-line supervisors were encouraged to institute programs to alleviate problems in their zone areas. Both services reported an increased flow of suggestions from patrol officers since shifting to a community-based policing mode. Promotions and transfers of police personnel were reported as taking into account the performance and initiative of the individual constables in promoting the interests of the communities they serve.

Services A and C police tended to have a very informed view of community composition, evidenced by their various experiences at attempting community input. Service-A, for example, polled the community in 1989 by means of a public needs survey in an attempt to gauge community attitudes toward the service they were providing. They subsequently met frequently with various interest groups and community representatives, imparting information regarding their five-year plan, for example, or results from the public needs survey.

Service-B focussed community consultation efforts on close contact with members of selected organised interest groups in the community. Senior officers participated as committee members of various community groups, especially visible minority and gay and lesbian interest groups. These contacts seemed to have a good deal to do with sentiments of members of the police board. The chairperson of the Service-B police board stressed that the first link in the communications chain between the community and the police was the police services board. This link was nurtured by inviting minority community members to public meetings where individuals met members of the police services board.

Service-B had also established four police–community centres, in collaboration with and dependent upon financing from local area business. The goal of this program was to have the centres managed by a volunteer board of directors, with day-to-day operations handled by community volunteers. It was hoped that these centres would provide a vehicle for community opinion and information to Service-B. However, the centres were manifestly police driven, without the necessary support from the communities to become high traffic sites or locally managed.

In general, there were many opportunities for the three police agencies to engage in public consultation. However, these appeared to be wasted as the police personnel were more concerned with providing the public with police output of information. For example, respondents more often spoke about being invited to speak at community groups, schools, and homeowners associations, and the opportunity to thereby represent the police service and its point of view. Police personnel did not even appear to take advantage of the potential information that could be provided by community members attending these functions, by addressing questions to them.

Nevertheless, attempts to structure the information entering the police organisation from the community into a useable format were being made in the two community-based services. Service-A implemented a system in which quarterly reports were produced by each platoon, in order to inform senior management about the issues in each community. In Service-C, a zone operated with a community advisory committee. Minutes were kept and circulated as were incident reports, and both were available for regular meetings of patrol officers in a zone, or to the daily meetings of senior officers and zone commanders. However, the minutes, and especially the incident reports, appeared spartan in content and, by and large, related to offenses.

Also, technology was found to afford some enhanced, albeit limited, information links with the public in these two police services. Service-C employed a computer-generated voice mail system to maintain contact with community advisory committee members. Messages and meetings agenda, for example, were routinely conveyed by means of the system. Service-A used an internal computer information network, but only for in-house organisational communications such as notifying personnel regarding policy changes, or notifying and inviting zone personnel to attend upcoming community meetings.

Most impressive in S–A were the constables' descriptions of the process they followed when submitting reports on the internal network. This system allowed the person submitting the report to designate all those who should receive the report, as well as those who should respond to it. For instance, if the constable wanted the involvement of the youth section, then they would flag the youth section on the attached activity log. Every section or individual who received a copy of the report had to clear the report before it was removed from the activity log. The system not only allowed for the structuring and streamlining of internal agency communications but also the conveyance of information within the organisation since personnel were accustomed to logging on routinely. It was, however, an internal police information system, and the system was not designed to incorporate social events and preventive data for police nor to share information with the public.

In summary, all three police services were attempting initiatives in establishing community contacts. The contacts had in turn been understood as opportunities to intervene in and to influence the communities with improved information as to police policies and operations. It was also understood in each of the services that the community links should permit improved information for the police services. It was evident, however, that the police agencies did not take advantage of the opportunities to garner public feedback. Consequently, community relations, similar to media relations, could be described as heavily weighted toward police output of information.

Public Complaints

Public complaints may be considered feedback to a police service, as well as being an opportunity to respond to concerns and objections of community members. Investigation of public complaints in the three police services was the responsibility of a specifically designated officer of the rank of staff sergeant or sergeant. The process appeared to present a high degree of operational feedback. Command rank personnel, and eventually supervisors, were kept informed of specific complaints investigations, and also used the process as a sensing device for difficulties, such as front-line morale or public impressions of police appearance and conduct.

General feedback to the public, however, was slight. Regular statistical reports were necessarily provided to police services boards, and in Ontario also to the Public Complaints Commissioner. But neither the boards nor the Commission advised the public in any way of the nature or significance of investigations completed and complaints resolved.

The nature of most complaints would allow for some statistical reporting to the public — and probably to the advantage of police services. While media attention to public complaints tends to focus upon the sensational incident, and thereby conveys a negative and distorted image of police conduct, real day-to-day police contacts with the public tend to generate rather more banal complaints. In fact major incidents such as alleged excessive use of force are not statistically representative. Most public complaints have to do with demeanour and alleged abuse of authority relating to what several respondents in our three case services referred to as "attitude problems." The other common complaints had to do with disreputable conduct and failure to act in response to a public demand. Often they were complaints that could be remedied by a thoughtful response from an officer concerned. When not, they were usually amended following the intervention of a complaints officer.

Complaints may at times point not only to the need for training police officers but also for better information to the public in regard to police discretion and authority. This may be especially true of immigrant or minority communities, whose experience of policing may differ from that of Canadian-born individuals. No such complaints-informed public feedback was found, however, in the three services examined, even though there was some indication that complaints officers had made an effort to keep individual complainants advised of their efforts. In Service-C, in addition to oral feedback to a complainant, it was normal to have the report read by the complainant, a practice which the police considered time-saving. Thus, even as the relationship was, by definition, one prompted by a disgruntled member of the public, there was some under-exploited opportunity to impress upon a complainant that a concern had been seriously and competently pursued.

It was remarked in each jurisdiction that there was far more disclosure now to the complainant, including opportunity to read written reports, and that this had had the consequence of actually reducing investigative time; indeed, the interaction had had a mediating effect. Also, as observed in S-C, there was often satisfaction and increased public confidence, despite the negative origins of the process. Feedback to the public, and at least to a complainant, may be viewed as an integral and normal part of a complaints investigation process, yielding a form of community relations.

In S-A, there was some increase in the number of public complaints in the initial years of community policing. If one thinks of complaints as a form of communication and information, one might consider that complaints increased with public confidence in the openness and fairness of the process. Moreover, since the bulk of public complaints had to do in some way with the demeanour of police officers, these could inform supervisory and training practices, and thereby generalise to improved police-citizen interactions.

The increased formality of the complaints procedure was remarked in all of the jurisdictions considered, but especially in Ontario. In the view of some respondents, legislated procedural requirements introduced in 1993 had taken complaints out of the hands of the community. With an emphasis on formal complaints, concern was expressed that the process has become more incident-driven, less amenable to informal resolution and perhaps less responsive to real public needs. The brochures describing public complaints procedures were now entrusted to the provincial government in Ontario, and were made available in ten languages, although they were not conspicuously available to the public in the buildings of the two police services, S-A and S-B.

In the two Ontario services, the Police Services Act led to the explicit establishment of Professional Standards Bureaus. Previously in Service-B, only as recently as 1985 had an "internal affairs" designation been established to replace the previous practice of the chief delegating investigative tasks. In S-A, until 1990, the procedure had consisted of delegating to a selected investigating officer. In both of the services there was some sense that the new internal investigations of complaints was competently conducted, more so than in the not-too-distant past when there were no distinguishable complaints investigations personnel or clear procedures that were in keeping with legitimate expectations of professional standards.

In each service, too, the police officer in charge displayed personality characteristics that suggested an ability to finesse the delicate task of balancing professional investigations, public interest, and collegial relations. In none of the cases was the investigatory process so removed or abstracted as to represent some sort of covert operational threat to the serving police officers. Rather, the investigating officers appeared to have the capacity to interact informally, and thereby, even as they might within formal guidelines find against a police officer, be able to inform and advise people about conduct and public expectations. In each of the police services the process appeared to have the confidence of individuals and of the police association; the association, or union, had information access from officers under investigation and also, if sought, from the complaints officer. There was not a similar confidence, however, in provincial investigations, as these were perceived to be politically motivated, exceedingly slow, non-informative, and consequently damaging to the morale of a police officer under investigation.

While public complaints or internal disciplinary investigations were necessarily highly confidential while underway, there was indication in each service that the internal affairs officers were accorded broad-ranging access to all personnel in addition to priority reporting access to the deputy chiefs and the chief. In so doing, therefore, the officer in charge of complaints was able to offer informal advice to officers on behaviour, perhaps in resolution of a complaint. But additionally, where there was indication of a systemic problem associated with some number of similar complaints, the complaints officer was able to seek policy, supervisory, or training amendments.

While this reflexive function did appear to occur in each of the three services, it may also be noted, nonetheless, that it was in each instance somewhat *ad hoc* rather than systematic. There was little indication of an overview of complaints internal to any of the three services. On the other hand, in S–C, which had a strong internal training capacity, there was indication that the complaints investigation process was especially useful to the training officer in informing in-service course content.

In summary, in each of the police services public complaints were managed on the basis of formal protocol while still permitting a non-trivial measure of informal mediation or solution and feedback. While the process appeared effective for both complainants and police officers, it was evident that there was no systematic analysis of complaints information for purposes of policy, operations, or training. Nor was there any generalised feedback to the communities during or following a completed investigation.

Conclusions

Police services are quite evidently sporadically intent upon delivering information to the public. The information tends to be delivered in a fashion that defines the public as being passive or, in a sense, on a need-to-know basis. Moreover, there is still an emphasis upon limiting information and that information still tends to be skewed in the direction of crime reporting. The service-related functions and opportunities afforded police officers tend not to be conveyed, in part because they are less likely to be reported by the media.

Illustratively, in 2002 in Ottawa a case leading to the dismissal of an Ottawa constable was critically reported a month after the investigation. The critical tone occurred precisely because the public had been unaware of the misconduct inquiry. Members of the service fretted that informing the public of the constable's behaviour would damage public perceptions of their service (*Ottawa Citizen*, January 29, 30; CBC Radio News, January 29, 30). Subsequently, a press editorial lamented the absence of effective notice and information release (*Ottawa Citizen*, January 31, 2002) and the services board, claiming that had they looked the press would have seen notices of proceedings, announced they would look into better press liaison (*Ottawa Citizen*, February 1, 2002).

Insofar as information input, it is a recurring observation that police services improvise in the utilisation of information available to them. There is a wealth of data available from front-line and command-rank contacts with the public, and from the direct contacts associated with media and community relations and from complaints procedures. Although it is undoubtedly advisable that police implement additional information collection measures, it is evident that even the information normally available is not being analysed.

A community field intelligence unit for the collection and analysis of data pertinent to both crime and preventive activities would enhance police effectiveness. The unit could conduct, or have a budget to contract for, public research, and could include systematic media-monitoring. These capacities need not be entirely in-house — and probably should not be, for reasons of cost-effectiveness. A co-ordinating or steering capacity could exist within the organisation, but a good deal of the analysis or ancillary information gathering could be contracted out. Some explicit collaboration with public data gathering/analysis bodies, including Statistics Canada, could be managed. This capacity would deal not only in crime-related data but also in social information that would inform prevention as well as predict offences.

Regular provision of in-service training courses directly derived from community intelligence analysis could be a feature of police services, whether operating individually or in collaboration with other regional services and public educational institutions. The latter collaboration, with community groups and private and public educational bodies, is highly favoured, as it in itself is an interactive or reflexive information-gaining process.

These observations occur in a continued period of some philosophical and organisational change. The three case police services, as most others in Canada, were variously engaged in the continuing, perhaps stalled, transition away from traditional reactive law enforcement culture and para-military structure to community policing. Consequently, there was some indication (varying in degree among the services) of a shift to improved lateral and vertical communications within the organisations, and improved communications with the public. Yet, the para-military inhibition on communications persisted, expressed in continued dependence upon formal and written communications, internally and externally, and a tendency to favour control of information flow to the public, in a one-way emphasis that enhances the police role as expert. Moderation of this fault was associated with the extent of community policing.

A commitment to community-based policing involves a change in philosophy on the part of the police organisation to sharing priority and policy decision-making with the community. In order to ensure appropriate community input police organisations need to listen to the entire community. Police organisations could be more effective in reaching out and heeding their communities if they pro-actively managed information exchanges. In doing so, the quality of information gained by police services — if shared rather than hoarded by individuals, and if analysed and used to inform policies and actions — would enhance policing at all levels, from "broken windows" (Wilson and Kelling, 1982) to national and international crime.

Five

Big Policing

Dennis Forcese, David Horne, Nancy Lewis-Horne

Introduction

Is big better? Politicians seem to think so. Large organisations, whether city governments, hospitals or police services, are presumed to involve economies of scale. Even during decades of rhetoric about community-based services and community accountability the experience in Canada has been of organisational mergers. In contrast to the decentralisation associated with community policing, and the emphasis upon local accountability, the merger of organisations may possibly in itself be a contradiction and an impediment to community policing. There is little empirical evidence to suggest that expected fiscal economies will be realised, and in fact, a good deal of contrary evidence suggesting that the initial costs of reconciling sub-units often mortgages future budgets. Greater distance between police and citizens may be expected. Bureaucratic layers are apt to increase, and more personnel are likely to be removed from direct service delivery. Animosities and competition may be introduced from the merging units, leading to failed cooperation and information exchange. Months, even years may be devoted to integrated work practices, communications, and collective agreements, detracting from other organisational objectives.

This chapter surveys literature related to the regionalisation or consolidation of police services in urban areas. Of the available research, much is from the United States. Generally this chapter attempts to depend upon such research rather than anecdote and opinion passing for evidence. We are all familiar with some such opinion and anecdotal information, often reported as a citizen perception of loss of police services (Forcese, 1999:91–94) The following discussion, however, seeks to consider outcomes in addition to citizen perception of policing, and focusses on bureaucratisation, service effectiveness, and economies.

Economies of Scale

Even as there are data that suggest a diminished level of police service in larger organisations, probably more persuasive to political policy makers is the anticipation of economies inherent in size. Research suggests, however, that these economies are elusive. Consider some of the costly circumstances following a merger. Invariably there are redundancies in organisational positions and incumbents, normally dealt with by way of buyouts and early retirements. In particular, at more senior administrative levels, not least chiefs and deputies, costly redundancies will either be tolerated without regard to efficiency, or bought out at some considerable cost, with the expenditures amortised into the future. Additionally, the new chief executive officer will often wish to be surrounded with his own appointees, usually promotions; the salary grid is therefore compounded. The new chief, too, if selected from one of the merging organisations, as will frequently be the case, may collect both severance and pension benefits contracted with the pre-merger organisation, plus a newly negotiated salary. Also, it is not uncommon to find people whose contracts are purchased at merger, especially skilled senior civilian personnel, later brought back on consultancy contracts to provide some of the institutional knowledge and skills that may have been lost. The several collective agreements of the merging units have to be reconciled. Rarely is this done quickly and rarely by means of reconciling to the lowest cost baseline; rather, one sees adjustments to the most favourable contract levels. Equipment and technology have to be reconciled, everything ranging from logos, stationery, and vehicle paint jobs to communications and computing. And these costs occur without any measure of the interpersonal costs and communications difficulties associated with the proliferation of employees to be integrated or the public relations burdens.

The consolidation of municipal services has been a topic of research from an economic perspective for over forty years (e.g., Hirsch, 1959; Tiebout, 1960). Generally, the discussions involve whether or not metropolitan areas are operated and administered more efficiently and effectively by a consolidated governmental structure or by a fragmented system of jurisdictions. It is often *assumed* that the duplication involved in the fragmented jurisdictions leads to inefficiency and increased costs in municipal government. This is a view *not* supported by research (Ostrom and Parks, 1973). Studying police service delivery in Indianapolis researchers concluded that "larger jurisdictions consume a larger

share of resources than smaller ones serving similar neighbourhoods" (389). As the size of the area to be policed increases, there
is an increase in per capita expenditures on police services (Ostrom and Parks, 1973). This increase in expenditures was not reflected in an increase in service: "For constant service levels, a decrease in the relative number of police departments in a metropolitan area is associated with higher costs per capita" (Ostrom and
Parks, 1973:390).

Organisational Size and Bureaucracy

Some insight into the operational consequences of an organisation's size can be gleaned by examining existing police services.
It is not unexpected, of course, that the larger the organisation,
the greater the bureaucratic layering. As remarked in previous
chapters, "de-layering" is one of the measures required in making a transition to community policing. Revealing work was conducted in Nova Scotia. Murphy (1986) analysed the influence of
bureaucratic form on the delivery of police services in Nova Scotia through a comparative analysis of ten RCMP detachments and
thirty small-town independent police organisations. He found the
RCMP detachments to be more bureaucratic than their municipal counterparts when comparing five organisational indicators
(1986:106): centralisation or top–down emphases in decision-
making; formalisation or an emphasis upon rule-bound service —
"doing-it-by-the book;" police professionalism, or an emphasis
upon detachment from citizens as a means to objectivity; organisational closure, or an isolation from other agencies; and task specialisation, or a segmentation of roles and responsibilities. Only
the last, specialisation, was not significantly greater in the RCMP
detachments as contrasted to the municipal services. Murphy also
found that centrally controlled RCMP detachments set their operational goal in terms of crime (the reduction of certain types of
offences) and that "formal rules, procedures, policies and operational standards" are set by policy makers removed from the
community (236). As a result of centralised policy-making "detachment commanders have little organisational incentive to rad-
ically adjust police policies to meet local demands" (238).

In contrast, most municipal departments studied by Murphy
had low levels of formal bureaucratic structuring. He states that
"municipal police chiefs recognise the necessity of maintaining
visible organisational access to the community and readily acknowledge that community groups have a legitimate role in in-

fluencing their departments policies and procedures" (1986:247). This observation is supported by his finding that the bureaucratic form of the police organisation determined the way in which minor liquor offences were dealt with: municipal police organisations handle such incidents largely through informal means while the RCMP usually proceeds by laying charges (251).

For other criminal incidents, Murphy found similar results: the RCMP employ criminal charges while small agencies rely on informal methods. He also determined that "seven out of eight crime rate categories are significantly and positively correlated to police bureaucratisation ... [this] suggests a strong relationship between public bureaucratisation and reported crime rates and supports the general hypothesis that the more bureaucratic a police department becomes, the more it is likely associated with a higher recorded crime rate" (1986:285). Consequently, Murphy suggests crime statistics are indicators of organisational characteristics (i.e., formal and informal approaches to recording crime) as opposed to true indicators of criminal activities or measures of officer productivity. Put otherwise, crime statistics reflect the character of a policing organisation and not necessarily the character of a community. Nor do the crime statistics, as a measure of police effectiveness, translate into fundamental crime fighting in the sense of prevention and the economies that might be taken to be associated with preventive and diversionary solutions that do not invoke the criminal justice system.

Associated with these basic features, it is evident that the larger the organisation the more difficult it is to actually implement reform intended to decentralise and innovate. Given that large police bureaucratic organisations are associated with centralised control of policy, innovations such as problem-oriented community policing are difficult to implement. Such innovations fly in the face of a management style learned within such an organisation and then expressed locally, as within an RCMP detachment. This management style is a function of learned experience, as well as an expression of continued managerial policy frameworks from the larger body. Moreover, any reform-oriented decentralisation challenges the power hierarchy and norms of internal accountability of the organisation at local and national levels.

As noted above, Murphy found that a large centralised police bureaucracy controlled the flexibility of local police administrators by framing policy and adherence to bureaucratic requirements. He notes: "detachment administration is carried out, but ultimately not controlled, by the local detachment commander"

(1986:236). Regarding the detachment commander, Murphy suggests "while he may have some flexibility in interpreting and applying centrally derived policies, this depends on clearance from a higher level of authority within the organisation" (236–237). The consequence is a "force first, community second philosophy ... an inevitable result of a centrally administrated police bureaucracy" (240).

Murphy relates an example of a community-based team policing experiment initiated by an innovative RCMP detachment commander. The experiment was allowed to operate:

> until it became clear that it conflicted with organizational policies ... [the commanding officer was] replaced with a more traditional 'by the book' commander who reinstated a strict policy based model stressing internal accountability and not community accountability. This was done despite the community's publicly stated wish to keep the previous commanding officer and his community model. (1986:239)

Resistance to change in police organisations has been documented in many studies (Germann, 1971; Sherman, 1975; MacLagan, 1987; Schwartz and Clarren, 1977). Change and innovation within police organisations has been called "the impossible dream" (Germann, 1971) or compared to "bending granite" (Guyot, 1977). However, despite these findings many advocates of community-based policing (e.g., Webber, 1991; Normandeau and Leighton, 1990) argue for the decentralisation of authority and power to enable those at the lower levels of the police organisation to respond to community problems facing them. Unfortunately, such innovations challenge the formal and informal power structures of the police organisation (Kelling, 1978:179).

The formal power structure of police bureaucracies is characterised by the rank system, where sworn officers begin their police careers as constables and have the potential to be promoted through the ranks of sergeant, staff sergeant, inspector, and upwards. There appears to be a positive relationship between the size of the police organisation and the potential for promotion: as the organisation gets larger, so does the number of ranks and the number of positions within ranks. For example, Bayley (1991:41) observes that in most Canadian major cities, divisions or districts are commanded by superintendents as compared to RCMP detachments of similar size, which are commanded by sergeants. This example demonstrates that commanding rank is not related to the amount of responsibility of the position but rather to organisational characteristics such as size.

The rank system influences the introduction of innovation. According to Bayley (1991) local commanders have limited discretion (in terms of amount and latitude) over the deployment of resources. Further, local commanders are judged by their superiors in terms of crime and clearance rates, "adherence to procedures of the department, 'staying out of trouble,' and maintaining appropriate behaviour from the rank and file" (1991:42). In referring to innovation, Bayley states:

> Initiative can be displayed only after commanders have answered calls-for-service, investigated crimes, and kept discretionary enforcement at acceptable levels. Adaptation to local needs, which one hears so much about, occurs only after these priorities are met. (1991:42)

Consequently, should a local commander display innovation and not attend to these organisational requirements, the power structures are threatened, and as Murphy (1986) has found in the RCMP, the innovations are at risk.

Effectiveness

Without regard to reform, even within the frame of traditional policing, there is an interesting relationship between size and effectiveness. In essence, a police service can be either too small or too large. There appears an optimal size where breadth of service can be offered with reasonable economy without being impeded by bureaucratic layering. American research conducted in three major metropolitan areas and replicated in two other locations demonstrated that police agencies of medium size performed better on a range of indicators than did small or large police agencies (Ostrom et al., 1978b:45). Small agencies were defined as employing less than eleven full-time officers; medium as employing eleven to seventy-six full-time officers; and large as employing more then seventy-six full-time officers. The indicators used to measure effectiveness included victimisation rates, response rates, and citizen knowledge of police mistreatment.

The authors note that citizen responses have been most favourable in regards to small- and medium-sized police departments, as compared to similar neighbourhoods policed by larger agencies. The authors found "[i]n no instance did the larger departments studied perform more effectively across the full range of indicators included" (Ostrom et al., 1978b:45). Consequently, the empirical evidence that exists points to medium-sized departments as being optimal for police effectiveness. Findings from a national study of 102 cities also supported these results (Ostrom and Parks, 1973:382–383).

Research findings also document that organisational size influences service delivery in the fundamental number of persons available for street-level work. In particular, the larger the police organisation, the fewer the officers patrolling, especially at night. Evidence suggested that size of police agency influenced the deployment of personnel resources (Ostrom et al., 1978a:85). "[T]he larger the local police agency that produces patrol service, the lower the proportion of the agency's officers generally assigned to patrol duties" (Ostrum et al., 1978b:39). This negative relationship occurred as a result of the larger police agencies utilising officers to perform auxiliary and administrative services other than patrol-related duties. As a result, agencies with more than 150 sworn officers employed, assigned 55 percent of their officers to patrol, while those agencies with 51 to 150 sworn officers employed, averaged 63 percent of officers assigned to patrol (1978b:39).

Although larger police agencies have more police officers per 1,000 residents, servicing the additional requirements of the larger agencies resulted in reduced patrol officer availability than in the smaller police agencies. The result of consolidating small- and medium-sized police agencies could be to "increase, rather than decrease costs", or at the very least adjust to an increased citizen-to-patrol officer ratio (Ostrom et al., 1978a:85).

A consequence of an increased citizen-to-patrol officer ratio is lengthened response times for citizen service, from patrol officers, or at best, differential patrol priorities ill understood by the public. This circumstance is aggravated in that larger departments (those with over 150 sworn officers) employ two-person patrol crews more often than small- and medium-sized police agencies (Ostrom et al., 1978a:91). Consequently, the larger agencies, with their larger citizen-to-patrol officer ratio, will have an even smaller presence in the community as they will field fewer patrol units to respond to citizens' requests for assistance:

> Consolidated patrol arrangements are not necessarily better, however. Our data show that consolidation of small municipal patrol suppliers might in fact have a negative impact on patrol service to residents of the consolidated areas. We find that larger departments do

not translate their relative personnel advantage into as high an on-street presence as do the small-and medium-sized agencies. We also find that when staffing of patrol units (i.e., one-or two-officer patrols) is taken into account, the larger departments are even more thinly spread. (Ostrum et al., 1978a: 101)

Conclusions

We are very dependent upon rather dated American research, and in particular that of Ostrum and colleagues (1973, 1978a, 1978b), for systematic information on the consequences of large police organisations. These data have not been invalidated by any subsequent research and are intriguing, for they are congruent with a non-systematic aggregation of negative impressions from press reports relating to organisational mergers. And they are not contradicted by any evidence of improvements, even as the ideology of some government leaders insist that such is an outcome. We may conclude with the words of the American researchers:

> The findings from the studies discussed above do not lead us to recommend the elimination of large police departments serving metropolitan areas. However, they do lead us to question the accepted wisdom that policing in metropolitan areas will be improved by the elimination of all small police departments. A mixture of large and small agencies producing complementary service within a police industry may be a better organisational solution to the problem of metroplitan policing than the creation of large police monopolists who must themselves produce a wide variety of different police services to meet the diverse demands of heterogeneous populations living in most metropolitan areas. (Ostrum et al., 1978a:181)

Six

The Politics of Police Unions

Dennis Forcese

Introduction

In this brief chapter we offer a cautionary tale. It is an account of an atypical Canadian police employee group resorting to American police union tactics and of odd affiliations of provincial and municipal politicians and police union leadership. It is also an illustration of a crisis in public relations and public confidence in the police created by the antics of a police body beyond the control of management.

Police unions have been around for a long time in Canada, with quite militant examples in the post-World War I period, and a proliferation of such employee groups in the 1960s, culminating in employee organisations in all major police services in Canada. The conspicuous exception, of course, is the RCMP, reminding one of its traditional legitimation function in loyal subordination to the senior government.

Police associations in Canada have often overtly contested the authority of chiefs of police in cities as diverse as Moncton, Ottawa, Guelph, Niagara, Winnipeg, Edmonton, and Vancouver (Forcese, 1980, 1999). In the Montreal Urban Community, for example, the Police Brotherhood had often publicly contested — with some success — management decisions of which they disapproved, as in 1981, when they opposed the chief's intended dissolution of the riot squad (*Montreal Gazette* website, July 23, 1981). In the Niagara Region Police in 2000 the association overwhelmingly voted non-confidence in the chief. The vote was described in the media as a textbook tactic to "weaken or topple the chief." Two months later the Police Services Board asked the chief to stand down (*National Post*, January 17, 2000). As emphasised in workshops attended by Canadian police association representatives, the associations exist for the "accumulation and use of power" (*National Post*, January 17, 2000). But rarely, one might say never, has a Canadian police employee group been as outspoken and overt in its influence upon public opinion, politicians, and police management as the Toronto Police Association in the 1990s.

Union Politics in Toronto

Intermittent police association engagement in Toronto politics began before the 1990s. A prominent Toronto casualty of police opposition was Mayor John Sewell. The association publicly opposed the mayor following his having made statements about racism in the police service. The association had earned some reputation for homophobia and racism by virtue of published comments in the 1970s in its periodical *News and Views*. Sewell was not re-elected, and went on to lecture and write a book on policing (1985).

Arguably association actions up to and including the 1990s were particularly well reported because of the attention of one newspaper committed to aggressive police reporting, the *Toronto Star*. Through the decades and into the 1990s the association had layered its reputation with an explicit intent to take on politicians whom the association considered undesirable. But in the 1990s the association seemed to take their game to a new level, noticed by media beyond the *Star*, when they secured advice from their Los Angeles counterparts, and committed to taking on managers and politicians. Television and print media documented the association president confirming consultation with his Los Angeles counterpart, and seeking to topple civic politicians deemed hostile to police interests. The Toronto association president acknowledged that his group was intent upon hiring private investigators to search for incriminating information on politicians perceived to be opponents or critics of the police (*Montreal Gazette*, February 2, 2000).

One Toronto city councillor who publicly spoke of what she considered union harassment found her resignation being demanded by the union. The union requested that the Ontario Police Commission investigate Councillor Judy Sgro on grounds that she had not yet taken a mandatory training course for police service board members. The councillor had previously criticised the union of targeting politicians and in so doing, used a rather flamboyant comparison (for which she subsequently apologised), speaking of "something you'd see in Louisiana, where you daren't ask the police anything or you'll be found dead in the back of a car a week later" (*Toronto Star*, September 7, 1998).

Police: Selected Issues

Perhaps the high — or low — watermark in this ongoing process in Toronto insofar as public attention goes occurred in 2000 when the association embarked upon its "True Blue" campaign. The campaign against politicians and presumably others, such as police managers (*Montreal Gazette*, February 5, 2000) became infamously prominent with this association fund-raising campaign. The union stated that some of the money would be used in its lobbying to amend the Young Offenders Act, and to assist in creating a national DNA bank (CBC News, February 4, 2000). It was understood by local politicians that the funds would aid in the union practice of targetting undesired politicians (*Toronto Sun*, February 5, 2000). The True Blue campaign funds, quoting an association spokesman, were to be applied in part to the development of a "database throughout Toronto that we can utilise at the push of a button and that will help us immensely when we decide to challenge those politicians who do not support us and/or help us elect those politicians who do" (Bobier, 2000).

To raise monies for its activities, which included defending members against charges, bringing lawsuits against critics, and opposing the election of undesired politicians, the association sought to raise funds from the public. Uniformed officers began selling stickers for $100, $50, and $25, which could be attached to vehicles. Additionally, telemarketers were employed. Police intimidation and potential favouritism quickly became themes in newspaper editorials and letters to the editors. Members of the public complained of possible favouritism for those displaying stickers. "Is our name going on a computer so that the next time we get pulled over the officer can determine who gets a ticket and who gets a warning?," wrote one letter writer to the *Globe and Mail* (January 25, 2000). The Civil Liberties Association weighed in, with its director demanding that the Ontario Solicitor General terminate the campaign (CBC News, January 27, 2000). Similarly, members of the Law Union of Ontario cited the action as a violation of the Ontario Police Services Act, noting especially the provision that "Even if not on duty and not in uniform, a police officer may not solicit or receive funds, or engage 'in political activity that places or is likely to place the police officer in a position of conflict of interest'" (*Globe and Mail* January 25, 2000).

The association counterview was that an officer seconded to the union was not so bound (*Globe and Mail*, January 26, 2000), a position apparently quite valid in light of a Police Services Act amendment passed by the Conservative government in 1998 that allowed solicitations by police if acting as an association representative. The amendment had been passed over the opposition of the Ontario Chiefs of Police Association (*Ottawa Citizen*, February 1, 2000).

The chief charged the union executive with discreditable conduct; municipal politicians, including the mayor, criticised the union and eventually became embattled. The Police Services Board appeared reluctant to intervene and was convinced by the city mayor to postpone action in order to allow him to negotiate with the union head (CBC News, January 27, 2000). He failed and found himself an outspoken antagonist. Mayor Mel Lastman had previously been understood to have a good working relationship with the union president — the CBC television program, *The Fifth Estate* (February 2, 2000), had shown the two hugging. The mayor became an outspoken critic and declared the association "completely out of control," demanding provincial legislation to curtail such "spurious" and damaging activities. He additionally stated that henceforth "because of the events of the last few weeks, I will not seek, nor will I accept, any endorsement from this police union executive" and urged a similar approach by other politicians to this "out-of-control union" (*Toronto Star*, February 4, 2000).

On January 29 the Police Services Board ordered the union to cease the campaign and passed an explicit bylaw banning telemarketing and fund-raising for political activities by any police officer (CBC News website, January 29, 2000). The city council, with many elected members feeling threatened by the promise of union-paid surveillance and political intervention, went on to pass a bylaw ordering the cessation of the campaign; the association challenged their legal right to do so.

Ultimately, the particular matter of the True Blue campaign was resolved by a deal in which the city council agreed to drop its bylaw prohibiting raising funds for political purposes, while the association in turn dropped its lawsuit against Toronto council (Bobier, 2000). Despite initial bluster about fighting opposition "all the way to the Supreme Court" (*Ottawa Sun*, January 31, 2000), the union terminated the campaign. Throughout the controversy the Ontario government, reputed to have close ties with the association, refused to criticise or intervene (*Ottawa Citizen*, February 1, 2000).

Association versus Management

At a public event well covered by the media, the premier of Ontario once greeted the president of the Toronto police association as the person who ran the Toronto Police, an ill chosen but revealing set of words. Into this environment, late in 1999 a new chief of police was named in Toronto. Julian Fantino, experienced as a chief of police and returning to the organisation in which he had served as a police officer, was widely thought to be a "cop's cop." The chief, like his predecessors, entered a police organisation where the union had for decades been an outspoken and highly visible representative of Toronto policing. He assumed office following a conspicuous conflict between the police association and his immediate predecessor, and amidst rumors of a deal with the Toronto Police Association leading to his appointment. Although this speculation was publicly denied by both parties, a prior meeting had apparently occurred (*Toronto Star*, December 1, 1999), perhaps indicating no more than a practical acknowledgment of the power of the association and its aggressive president, Craig Bromell. Earlier the association had explicitly opposed the candidacy of one of its own deputy chiefs, who appeared on television stating that he was afraid of the association president (CBC, *The Fifth Estate*, February 2, 2000).

Prior to the naming of the chief, while Julian Fantino was still chief of York Regional Police, there was speculation in the press that Fantino was a person once opposed but now favoured by the association (*Toronto Star*, November 18, 1999). The very fact that the Association views were a factor underlined its power, but additionally, the reasoning attributed to the association for shifting to a favourable view of the prospective chief had to do with an anticipated alliance between an aggressive union and a forceful chief expected to support his officers. The association was distressed by charges brought against members by the outgoing chief, and generally by the interventions of Ontario's police investigative body, the Special Investigations Unit (SIU). Additionally, it was expected that Chief Fantino would ally with the association in opposition to local politicians (*Toronto Star*, November 18, 1999). Fantino was known to be outspoken and somewhat active politically, with connections, as the union was understood also to have, with the Mike Harris conservatives. In fact, subsequently when in office in Toronto the chief was chastised by the media for addressing an Ontario Conservative Party conference in February 2000 (*National Post*, February 17, 2000).

By late 2001, however, even Chief Fantino was a target of the union, who allegedly perceived him as too diligent in sanctioning officers, although the charges at issue were carry-overs from the previous administration. The association also alleged that, in the context of ongoing proceedings against officers, he had made "irresponsible comments to the media about … members" (*Toronto Star*, November 23, 2001), even as what seemed to be of concern was the chief not adequately defending members. The association indictment represented the chief as harming the reputation of the Toronto police, perhaps an ironic indictment, given the negative publicity surrounding many of the union activities.

The union mobilised a non-confidence vote, putting the question to members: "After reviewing the chief's performance, do you have confidence in his leadership?" The review was informed by an eight-page pamphlet that accompanied the ballot, with topic headings such as "Two Faces of Chief Fantino" and "Chief's Campaign of Silence" (*Toronto Star*, November 23, 2001). 5200 ballots from a membership of 7000 sworn and civilian members were reported as having been filed, of which 89.9 per cent were negative (*Globe and Mail*, January 19, 2002). The Police Services Board declared the vote to be irrelevant, "vindictive," and Fantino himself described it as "mischief-making" (*Toronto Star*, January 5, 2002). By way of additional conflict, the chief had complained that the union was having him followed by private investigators (as politicians had complained), to which complaint, by way of denial, the association launched an $18 million lawsuit (*Toronto Star*, January 8, 2002).

Conclusions

The muddled and rather undignified saga of police politics in Toronto is quiescent as this chapter is written. Chief Fantino and the Police Services Board dismissed the association referendum as mischief, and the association president declined to demand the resignation of the chief. The other major actor, Mayor Mel Lastman, once portrayed as a fan of the association and shown on television greeting its president in the mayor's office, has never recovered from the True Blue campaign. By 2002, when he blundered into a highly publicised hand-shake with a member of the Hell's Angel, Lastman's resignation from the police services board was demanded by the association, despite a prior apology to police members (*Toronto Star*, January 16, 2002). Having appeared to contradict a major law-and-order target — biker gangs — the Toronto association indicated that they had received representations demanding the mayor's resignation from other police organisations: the Police Association of Ontario, the Canadian Police Association, and the National Association of Professional Police

Police: Selected Issues

Officers (*Toronto Star*, January 16, 2002). While the association reaction is itself not remarkable, it is once again noteworthy that its actions were made prominently public, in keeping with its aggressive practice of being a major public face of police in Toronto.

Through the course of these events, perhaps to an extent greater than witnessed during police strikes that have occurred in Canada, the media in the nation's media capital lambasted the Toronto police. The stories were carried nationally. Public impressions of Toronto police as a self-serving interest group rather than objective and dedicated peacekeepers contradicted the historic public view of Canadian police services. The association demonstrated its presence and power, and the public reputation of the police suffered.

Seven

Tactical Policing

Sam Alvaro

Introduction

The chapter offers a descriptive analysis of an overlooked trend in Canadian policing: the growth in number and shift in character of police tactical units. Since there are numerous police tactical units that go by a myriad of names (Special Weapons and Tactics, Emergency Task Force, Tactical Rescue Unit, Special Emergency Response Unit, Joint Task Force, etc.), these units, for the purposes of our discussion will all be called Police Tactical Units (PTUs). A survey of all police departments with fifty sworn officers or more provides the first comprehensive national data on PTUs in Canada. The chapter summarises data from a national survey (Alvaro, 2000) and documents a rise in the number of PTUs, an escalation in their level of activity, a normalisation of these units into mainstream policing, and a direct link between Canadian and American PTUs as well as the Canadian Armed Forces. These findings are similar to trends in the United States, suggesting that behind the rhetoric of democratic reforms such as community and problem-oriented policing, we are seeing the increased acceptance and resort to tactical law enforcement.

Currently, even as community policing is being celebrated as a return to Sir Robert Peel's policing principles, the military character of policing is finding renewed emphasis in police tactical units. Since development of the Los Angeles Police Department's tactical unit in 1967, the United States has seen an increase in the number of time these tactical units have been called upon to maintain order in its society. Some cases have ended in disaster, such as Waco, Ruby Ridge, and the Christian Movement for Life. At the same time, albeit to a lesser extent, Canadian society has also witnessed several widely publicised events involving police tactical units: Oka in Quebec (before the situation was turned over to the military), the Gustafsen Lake stand-off in British Columbia (where several Royal Canadian Mounted Police Emergency Response Teams were deployed to resolve the situation), and in Ontario at Ipperwash (where the Ontario Provincial Police Tactics and Rescue Units were called upon).

Distribution

As most would expect, the location pattern of these units follows the pattern of population centres in Canada. The units tend to be located around the largest census metropolitan areas and there are police tactical units in every province and territory. With the exception of a few provinces, there is more than one unit per province; five provinces have full-time units and the remainder only part-time. Ontario has the majority of full-time units while British Columbia has the majority of part-time units. One surprising element in the geographical data shows that the province of Quebec does not have nearly as many PTUs when compared with other provinces of similar geographical size and population, such as Ontario or British Columbia.

There were several attitudinal questions asked of the tactical commanders who responded to the survey, questions concerning their views surrounding tactical policing. One hundred percent of the respondents answering the survey stated that tactical operation units are a vital part of modern policing and 98% agree that policing will become more tactical in the future. Hence, it is not surprising that, of the 83 police services surveyed, 65.1% (54 services) reported having a police tactical unit. When examined by population size, with few exceptions, jurisdictions serving a population larger than 101,000 currently maintain a unit. On the other hand, in those areas of 51,000–100,000, less than half (46.7%) have PTUs and in the smallest population groups, under 51,000, only 30.8% of the police services have such a unit.

Full- and part-time units

Thirty-seven percent of the 54 police services operate PTUs on a full-time basis and 55.6% on a part-time basis; the remaining 7.4 percent are multi-jurisdictional units that work in conjunction with one or more police services in either full- or part-time capacity. Full-time tactical officers devote all their time solely to tactical unit duties while part-time officers may work in any number of other capacities within the department, from traffic duty to supervisory positions. When needed, part-time officers would be called upon to form the tactical unit and help to resolve the situation at hand.

In total there are 84 PTUs in Canada. Of the four provinces with full-time units, the majority are in Ontario (42.6%), followed a distant second by British Columbia (11.1%), then Alberta (9.3%), and lastly Quebec (7.4%). It is important to point out that some police services with jurisdictions in major metropolitan centres or, for example, provincial police and RCMP divisions serving relatively vast geographic areas, maintain more than one unit to provide an adequate and efficient response to situations that may require a PTU.

Police services without a tactical unit

Several respondents indicated that should they require assistance they would request a unit from a neighbouring police service. In fact, many of the police services that do not have a unit have an agreement in place with a neighbouring police service to deal with such situations. Through the course of interviewing the respondents and collecting data it was discovered that each time these units are "borrowed" the police service requesting the unit is billed for the use of the unit. The majority of police services that do not have a PTU of their own tend to rely upon larger police services such as the RCMP, or in Quebec and Ontario, upon the provincial police PTUs.

The majority (86%) of police services without a PTU were found to be serving population centres under 100,000; however, there were several police services whose jurisdictions exceeded 100,000 and who were also without a PTU. When some of these police services were contacted, reasons given for not having a unit included a lack of funding and that agreements were already in place with larger police services in case a PTU was needed. Only two of the police services without a PTU (N = 29) were planning to set up a unit of their own and were expected to be operational by 2002. When these new units become operational, there will be a total of 56 police services in Canada with a PTU.

Tactical unit features

Unlike their American counterparts, Canadian units do not use the politically charged acronym SWAT (Special Weapons and Tactics). In fact, fewer than 2% (N = 1) of the Canadian units surveyed use the name. The name that is most popular among Canadian teams is Emergency Response Team (41%); the next most popular name is Emergency Response Unit (10%). The rest of the police services used an array of names ranging from Emergency Task Force and Emergency Services Unit to Groupe d'intervention, Section technique, and Tactical and Rescue Unit, to name a few.

There are 54,722 police officers across Canada; of these, 1242 are tactical officers (CCJS, 1999); that is, some 2% of all police officers are part of tactical units. When unit status data are examined, full-time units have more than fifty percent of all tactical officers and, on average, have 34 officers per unit, while part-time units have 18 officers per unit. It is interesting to note that 55% of the police services replying reported an increase in tactical personnel since the beginning of the 1990s. Upon further analysis, it was found that, in the western provinces, part-time units, and units serving population centres between 51,000 and 100,000 were most likely not to have seen an increase in personnel.

Personnel

In contrast to the national figure, the survey data indicate that some police services have fewer than 1% of their total officers on the tactical unit, and some have as high as 20% (mean 5.7%) of their entire service in their tactical section. It was found consistently that the smaller the police service, the greater the percentage of tactical officers. This can be accounted for simply by noting that the average part-time tactical unit has 18 officers. Hence, when there are only 100 officers in the police service and a ten-man unit, then, that is already 10% of the total police service. All things being equal large police agencies that maintain full-time units have less than one half of one percent of all their officers in the tactical section.

As one might expect these units typically will have a member who has had prior military experience. Surprisingly — and of importance — is the fact that these units are more likely to have a female team member rather than an officer who has had Special Forces experience in the military. This datum on the surface is a definite departure from the United States hyper-masculine experience that is painted by Peter Kraska (1994) in his ethnographic research and the data of the 1997 survey (Kraska and Kappeler, 1997). One tactical commander commented: "There are police officers out there that have special operations experience, but they choose not to enter the tactical unit. I know of guys who were in the military that are now are doing traffic and investigations."

Table 1: Police Tactical Unit Demographics by Unit Status
(Alvaro 1999 survey results)

	Full-time Total		Part-time Total		Total	
	Mean	Sum	Mean	Sum	Mean	Sum
No. of officers in PTUs	34.21	650	18.40	552	23.88	1,242
No. of females	.45	9	.20	6	.30	16
No. of officers with military service	1.84	35	1.40	42	1.56	81
Military, Special Forces experience	.21	4	.20	6	.19	10
Prior experience with PTU	.50	9	1.10	33	.82	42
Years of service prior to PTU	8.21	N/A	6.77	N/A	7.44	N/A
No. of years in PTU	5.47	N/A	6.48	N/A	5.97	N/A
Average Age	33.78	N/A	34.53	N/A	34.20	N/A

Gender

Prior to the results presented here, it was considered that police tactical units were entirely a male phenomenon. Of the 58 police services that have such a unit, nine (15.5%) have between one and six females actively on the unit, for a total of 16 female tactical officers across Canada, translating into 1.2% of all tactical officers; this is far below the national average of 12.2% (N = 6,686) of female police officers in Canada (CCJS, 1999). While 1.2% seems to be insignificant, upon further analysis women: officers were found in a majority of provinces, at all population levels, and in both full- and part-time teams. In fact, the majority of women are in full-time units.

Prototypical tactical officer

The prototypical tactical law enforcement officer is a male, 34 years of age, who has had slightly over seven years of police experience prior to becoming a tactical officer, and is likely to remain a tactical officer for approximately six years but less than ten. This would imply then, that the typical tactical officer is an experienced police officer prior to entering the tactical unit and is dedicated enough to commit a sizeable portion of his career to tactical duties.

Police: Selected Issues

Rotation policies

Paul Ford, a tactical officer has said succinctly that:

> Within the rhetoric of community policing, officers in specialised units are being depicted as isolated and out of touch with real police work ... As SWAT officers, we should be willing to do our part so the concepts of Community Policing and SWAT can work together in harmony. However, some officers, particularly those in specialised positions, are finding it difficult, the primary reason for that difficulty seems to lie in one of the central goals of Community Policing, "to integrate all police services (patrol, investigation, etc.), with team members functioning as generalists." (Ford, 1995:42)

A mainstay of the community policing philosophy has been to have an officer that is more multi-faceted, a generalist, not an officer who is highly specialised in one aspect of policing. This has caused year limitations or mandatory rotation policies to be implemented by police services. By doing so the patrol officer is able to widen his skill-set and knowledge base.

To investigate how the generalist attitude of community policing has affected police tactical units, the question was asked if Canadian units have a policy of rotating their officers. The responses showed that almost half the units (45.3%) rotate their officers in and out of the tactical unit. This was higher for full-time units (55%) and lower for part-time units (36%). The range of years spent in rotation amongst the rotating officers fluctuated from a minimum of one year to a maximum of 12 years, the average being six years that an officer would stay active in the tactical unit.

Police Tactical Units Budgets

Close to 18 million dollars was spent in Canada on police tactical units in 1997; however, this figure does not include the salaries of the 1,242 tactical officers: "Police expenditures totalled 5.99 billion in 1997 ... In general, salaries and wages make up over 80% of the policing dollar" (CCJS, 1999:11-12). If we accept this formula, then less than one percent of all policing dollars in Canada is being spent on tactical units. This situation is reflected in the survey.

Some tactical commanders (2.7%) indicated that they did not have a tactical budget in 1997, while some reported that up to three percent of their total police budget was being allocated to

their tactical unit. In today's society of cost cutting, if the prototypical unit spends less then one percent of the total police
budget, under these conditions it makes sense for police exec-
utives to have a unit, when the rewards are so great. When all
levels of status are considered, the average unit spent slightly
over $400,000 in 1997. When broken down into unit status, how-
ever, full-time units spent over $1 million while part-time teams
spent only slightly over $54,000 per year. Over $16 million (91%)
of all tactical dollars being spent in Canada is being spent by 34.1%
(N = 15) of all tactical units, all of which are full-time. In particular, Ontario accounts for the majority of money being spent on
tactical law enforcement.

Yearly Formations

The first PTU in Canada was formed in 1968 in Toronto. This unit
was primarily designed to deal with civil unrest occurring at that
time and later became formalised into a tactical unit during the
early 1970s. With the exception of a few years in each decade since
the late 1960s there has been at least one unit formed every year in
Canada (Figure 1). There appears some increase in PTU formation
following the FLQ-related "October Crisis" (1970). But more pronounced, the data suggest that the Munich Olympics (1972) with
the terrorist actions against the Israeli athletes, and the Montreal
Olympics (1976) and security concerns related to the formation of
tactical units. There is a dramatic incrase in PTU formation in 1973,
lasting for 10 years. The survey shows that there was a substantial
rise in the formation of these units in 1974 and this growth continued until 1985. During 1974, two units were formed; the following
year three, then in 1976 six units. By 1976 almost 30% of all units
in service today had been formed; by 1980, the figure was 56%.
There was a greater increase during those four years than in all of
the 1980s. By the beginning of 1990, over 80% of units in service
today were up and running. After 1985 there was only one unit
formed per year until 1992 when there was a dramatic increase in
new units not seen since the seventies.

By 1997, the 54 separate police agencies in Canada had 84
tactical units (some police agencies have more than one). This
trend is similar to that found in the U.S. However, the rise in the
United States has not been as pronounced as that in Canada. Since
1986, the majority of units being formed in Canada have been
from police jurisdictions serving fewer than 250,000 people. Initially, it was thought that population size of the jurisdiction may

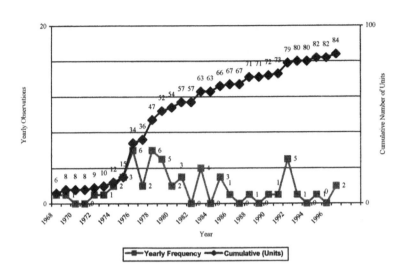

Figure 1: Annual Formation of Police Tactical Units since 1968
(Alvaro 1999 survey)

have been a factor in the formation of these units, but, on closer inspection of the data, population size does not appear to have played an important role.

Rationale for formation

It is necessary and important to look at why these units were formed in order to paint an accurate picture of the origins of Canadian tactical law enforcement. The data indicate there are four prominent rationales for the creation of a PTU (Figure 2). The most popular of which, was the occurrence of a high-risk situation (38.8%). One of the survey descriptions of a high-risk situation was:

> an increase in high risk situations such as hostage takings, man with gun etc. ... prompted the need for a team trained in special weapons tactics to resolve these matters. The general police membership possessed little training in dealing with these situations and were unequipped with the specialised tools required. (Alvaro Survey, 1999)

84

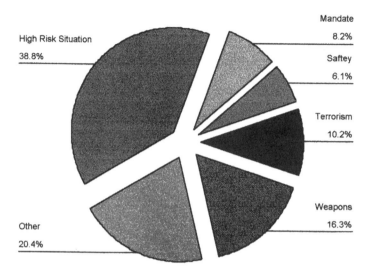

Figure 2: Rationale for Formation of Police Tactical Units in Canada (Alvaro 1999 survey)

The second most likely rationale for the formation of a PTU was situations involving weapons (16.3%); the third was terrorism (10.2%); and the fourth (8.2%) was an operational requirement by their police service or government to do so. There is no one rationale that seems to have precipitated the creation of a PTU. The most likely reasons during the 70s and 80s were terrorism and high-risk situations as well as an increase in weapons in the community. Nevertheless, upon further examination it appears that during the 1990s governments were beginning to mandate the formation of these units. One such example is the Ontario provincial government, which has required police agencies to have a PTU or enter into an agreement with another agency to have access to one.

Selection of Officers

To comprehend specifics regarding how officers are selected tactical commanders were asked to rank a set of criteria concerning the selection of their officers. These criteria ranged from psychological and physical fitness, to military experience, to education and seniority. The purpose of this question was two-fold: first, to see upon what basis are these officers selected for what 88% of respondents believed to be a prestigious position within their own department; and second, to determine (in light of American experience) how previous military experience and military special operations experience factored into the selection process of new officers. To shed some light on how the selection process works, in the interviews tactical commanders were asked how a regular officer would go about applying to become a tactical officer.

The officer must first send in his resumé and application to the tactical commander. In addition, some police services have certain basic requirement policies prior to application: in some cases, the officer must have a minimum number of years of police experience and meet rigorous physical fitness standards. Some police services also regularly recruit officers for the specific purpose of preparing them to become tactical unit officers, but this seems to be rare. Then the officer, depending upon the size of the department, will go through a series of interviews with not only the unit commander but also the tactical commander, squad leaders, and even with some team members. These interviews tend to centre around the individual's personality, to probe the officer about teamwork and ability to work in a team setting. Bearing in mind that police work traditionally lends itself to individual efforts, tactical units work in teams and it is imperative that these officers work well together.

The next level is the psychological examination stage; that is, is the officer a generally well-adjusted individual? If the officer successfully passes these phases, he or she must then go through a period of in-depth training, which differs widely depending upon the department. Some will make the officer take one month of 10–16 hours a day of training; others, as in the case of the RCMP, have a central training centre that offers a six-week course through which all of their tactical officers must pass. In the case of many of the smaller police departments, they will send their officers to a larger police service for training or bring officers in to their jurisdiction for instruction. In fact, one tactical commander interviewed said that he now has a small group of officers whose positions are solely dedicated to training officers inside and outside of his department.

The survey also found that 23 of the police services perform training with at least one other police service, a sign of cooperation amongst neighbouring police services. There are also units in place that send instructors from Ontario as far away as Nova

1.	Psychological fitness
2.	Physical fitness
3.	Firearms proficiency
4.	Performance on written or oral exam
5.	Seniority
6.	Education
7.	Military experience
8.	Special Operations experience in the military

Figure 3: Selection Criteria for Tactical Officers
(Alvaro 1999 survey)

Scotia; in several instances, Canadian officers have been sent to the United States to give instruction to American police officers. Upon completion of the applicant's initial training, the tactical commander takes one of two courses of action; the first is to keep the trainee on the unit as a new member of the team, and the second is to send the officer back to his or her original division. The latter choice does not necessarily mean that the officer has unsuccessfully completed his training or is inadequate to the task but it is possible that the unit may not have the requirement or the place for a new team member at such time. If the decision is made to keep the officer he will then go through a probationary period which varies from team to team. One tactical commander stated that his officers are always on probation. Throughout the probationary period, the officer is monitored closely and evaluated: relationship with the supervisor and the team, risk assessment, tenacity, motivation, stress, self-confidence, motivation, safety, and a host of other criteria are considered.

We asked tactical commanders to rank in descending importance certain criteria sought in a tactical unit officer (Figure 3). The results varied little when comparing full- and part-time teams, population of jurisdiction, or size of police department. Overwhelmingly, the most desired criterion in selection of a tactical officer is psychological fitness.

One tactical commander who regarded psychological evaluation as unimportant commented:

> For years we sent new applicants to be tested, they all came back fine. We felt that it was a waste of resources. In addition, what do you do with an officer who has been on the force for five or more years, then he fails the psyche test. This can cause a lot of problems, the officer's entire record must then be reviewed and then

you have to go back and ask, hey how did he get on the force in the first place? To get on the force you must go through a psyche exam we feel that is enough.

This review of psychological testing for tactical officers was a recommendation of the Drinkwalter Report (Ontario, 1989). The report found that in Ontario some of the psychological tests being used were thirty to forty years old and one self-administered test was dated 1922. While the above tactical commander makes a strong point, psychological fitness tends to be selected as the number one criterion in selecting a tactical officer. John Super (1995) did a study to see if certain psychological tests could distinguish between a "good" and "bad" tactical officer during the pre-employment phase. He discovered that "good" tactical officers scored high on femininity/masculinity scales, suggesting that they are more sympathetic and helpful. As one tactical commander put it, "ten years ago you might have had these macho types of officers on the unit, but no more. We need officers who can think and that have impulse control."

The next most valued criterion was physical fitness, followed by firearms proficiency and then performance on written or oral exams, seniority, and education. The criteria that were found to be least important were military experience and special operations experience within the military. This provides important evidence in Canada that while there has been a rise in tactical units and that they are becoming an increasing part of mainstream policing, they do not overly value military experience as a requirement for becoming a tactical officer.

Training

Training of these units also deserves mention, as it is a central component of their subculture. The survey asked how many hours per year a tactical unit actively spent in training: in total, Canadian PTUs collectively spend 21,493 hours a year for training purposes, and on average, each officer spends over 438 hours a year training. This is well over 200 hours beyond the training time of their American counterparts, who undergo on average 225 hours per year training (Kraska and Kappeler, 1997). This may suggest that due to the lack of importance placed upon military experience by Canadian tactical units, they may need to spend this amount of time training to learn military-type skills. When this is broken down by full- and part-time units, we find that full-time units

1.	Tactical operations unit training from another department
2.	Training provided by professional tactical schools
3.	Information from tactical units in the United States or Europe
4.	Book/videos/magazines/training manuals
5.	Police officers with experience in the military
6.	Training with active duty military experts
7.	Assistance or information from the Department of Justice
8.	Other

Figure 4: Sources of Training Expertise for Police Tactical Units
(Alvaro 1999 survey)

spend, on average, over 750 hours a year on training with some spending close to two thousand hours a year on training while part-time units spent 230 hours doing training. The least amount of hours being spent annually by a PTU was 72. With such a sizeable amount of time being spent on training, examination of this training becomes relevant.

In looking at the militarisation of these units, it was felt that the sources of training or expertise during the start-up period, as well as current sources, would reveal military or American connections. Tactical commanders were asked to list and rank the sources they currently or have previously used (Figure 4). These results varied little between full- and part-time units. Factors such as population of jurisdiction and size of the police service played only small roles, with the exception of some older teams who tend to conduct all their training in-house (14.8%; N = 8). This implies some police services do not require any of the sources listed and rely solely upon the resources within their own department. "Initially we went to the Canadian Military for training. Since then, we have relied on the expertise of 'other police' tactical units ... and our own experience, as well as training courses that become available." As one tactical commander stated, "we do not recognise military techniques as a priority in training. We find the use of in-house training as a better form of training." Another tactical commander who also conducts in-house training said, "We now do our own training expertise with instructor certifications received from varied sources. However, we still send officers to outside agencies for information purposes — to tactical schools."

Figure 4 provides very interesting results. The primary source of expertise reported was tactical operations unit training from another department. Of those surveyed, 55.5% (N = 30) had used a Canadian police service to train their tactical unit. Many of the larger police forces also provide training to smaller police services: the most predominate of these has been the Metropolitan Toronto Police Service (18.5% N = 10), the second being the RCMP (12.9%; N = 7). This suggests a similarity between the Metropolitan Toronto Police Service and the RCMP in Canada, and the Los Angeles Police Department SWAT team in the United States. Furthermore, the Toronto Emergency Task Force is a more popular source of training in Canada than the trans-national Royal Canadian Mounted Police. The second most popular source of expertise was training provided by professional tactical schools (20.3%; N = 12) such as the National Tactical Officers Association (12.9%; N = 7), and the gun manufacturer, Heckler and Koch (5.5%; N = 3). Third was information from tactical units in the United States and Europe. While no one listed any European police services, 22.3% (N = 12) indicated that they had trained with an American police service: the most common services to train with are the Los Angeles Police Department and the Federal Bureau of Investigation. It is very interesting to note that the Los Angeles Police Department, despite the distance, has a significant influence upon Canadian tactical policing. The next most popular sources of expertise were books/ videos/ magazines/ training manuals and then police officers with experience in the military. While training with active duty experts was ranked sixth overall, some very interesting results were found: a small percentage (16.6%; N = 9) had trained with the Canadian military and 5.5% (N = 3) had trained with the United States military; there was also one instance of training with the Navy SEALs and one instance of a unit training with the British Special Forces' Special Air Service Unit.

Tactical Deployments

The research indicates that a tactical call-out can mean many things. Some police services consider a tactical call-out to be an entire unit deployment, while others use the term when any one member is required for a situation. For example, one tactical unit commander has a team of two officers on a six-week deployment conducting surveillance operations: should this be considered a tactical call-out? When a tactical unit arrives on a scene of a hostage taking and the kidnappers give up after they are informed that the tactical unit is on the scene (which happens more frequently than most would think) is this a call-out? This raises an important issue: perhaps a nation-wide methodology should be developed to keep accurate and standardised records. Many police services were not able to give accurate numbers on either their call-outs or their activities. That being said, the number of call-outs made by these units can be a sign of their integration into mainstream policing. In 1980 units were being called out 24 times a year on average, that is, about twice a month. That number almost doubles by 1982 then dips well until the mid-eighties when it starts to increase again.

There is a dramatic increase in call-outs in 1993. If we look at the units that gave complete data, then the pattern in call-outs has been steady and does not decrease by more than 7 call-outs in any one year. Both sets of data indicate that these units, by 1997, are being called out approximately 17 times per month, that is, eight times the 1980 call-out rate.

While these units appear to be evolving into a normal part of police operations there is considerable difference between the full- and part-time units. In 1980, part-time units were being called out five times a year; by 1997, this had risen to 15 times, or just over one call-out per month. On the other hand, in 1980 the full time units reported 61 call-outs per year, about five times a month. By 1997, they were responding to 178 call-outs, translating into one call-out every other day. Subsequent analysis of the three largest cities revealed that those units on average conducted just over 400 deployments in 1997, that is, more than one deployment a day. This strongly suggests that these full-time units have already become part of everyday police operations.

Types of tactical deployments

The respondents were asked to break down their tactical activities into certain categories (Figure 5): barricaded situations (when a person has barricaded him or herself to prevent capture), hostage situations (when a person is being detained without his or her consent), terrorist activities, dangerous search/arrest warrants (these are situations were the persons named in the warrant are considered armed and or dangerous), civil disturbances, drug warrants, VIP security (at times these units provide security for dignitaries and politicians), and surveillance (one tactical commander indicated that, in certain circumstances, his people were better at surveillance, thanks to their training in concealment). Respondents were also allowed, in open-ended questions, to describe any additional activities that their unit may have undertaken in addition to those mentioned above.

There has been a marked change in the activities of these

91

Police: Selected Issues

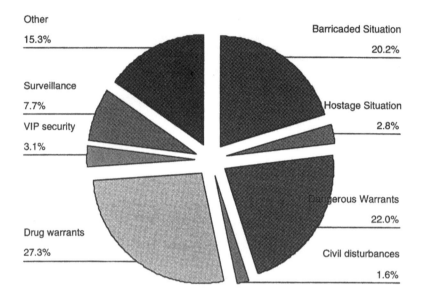

Figure 5: Canadian Police Tactical Unit Activities, 1997
(Alvaro 1999 survey)

units over time as they have taken on a more proactive role and as the scope of their roles has broadened. Half of the operations these units conduct (49.3%) are devoted to either drug (27.3%) or dangerous search/arrest (22.0%) warrants. The next most likely call-out for these units is for a barricaded situation (20.2%). Other call-outs included serving warrants for immigration and customs, aiding surveillance groups, and providing courtroom security and high-risk prisoner escorts. Canadian PTUs have conducted armed ship-boardings at sea, manhunts, and search-and-rescue operations for missing persons. In addition, they have provided witness protection; been involved with robberies, organised crime, and motorcycle gang situations; conducted high-risk vehicle stops; and intervened in suicide situations.

Such a range of PTU deployments leads to the following three observations: first, the mandate or traditional activities of the PTUs have widened; second, these officers provide a more specialised police service that seems to be needed; and third, these units appear now to spend more time in a proactive rather than reactive stance with respect to particular situations.

When the activities of these units are broken down into reactive and proactive categories, drug and dangerous search, arrests warrants, surveillance, and VIP security details are all proactive duties and represent 60.1% of PTU deployments. Reactive activities such as barricaded or hostage situations, and civil disturbances (which have been traditionally the role of these units) now account for only 24.6% of the operations they perform.

Pro-active Patrol

We have already seen that a large percentage of units are full-time, and there is an implication that many full-time units proactively patrol their jurisdictions. The survey discovered that 23% (N = 15) of the units responding were using their units proactively; furthermore, 20% (N = 3) were part-time units.

Most proactive units do not patrol with large numbers of officers; they are usually two- to four-man teams, spread out across a jurisdiction. For example, if there is a ten-man unit, it breaks up into three teams of two and one of four, with the supervisor included in the four-man team. These four teams of the tactical unit will be sent into four different quadrants of the jurisdiction in the interests of wider-spread patrol. In this configuration, a two-man unit can resolve many situations on its own, with the rest of the unit prepared as back-up, if required. When in their vehicles, the officers monitor police broadcasts and if they feel that their presence may be required, they then proceed directly to the scene to assess the situation. As noted earlier, these units do not necessarily belong to large jurisdictions; they may range from police services with jurisdictions as small as 51,000 to population centres accounting for over a million people. As one tactical commander put it: "It made good sense, this avoids the 'fire hall syndrome'" (the process of continuous training while waiting to be called out to an incident, without regular practical, hands-on experience).

Not all units became proactive immediately after their formation. Several units did became proactive in the same year in which they were formed during the 1970s but, notably, during the 1980s, no units began proactively patrolling their jurisdictions immediately (see Figure 6). The majority of proactive units began this practice during the mid to late 1990s, coinciding with the rise in formation of PTUs.

Some Comparative Commentary

Some comparative observations are possible with an informative American source (Kraska and Kappeler, 1997). In Canada, only

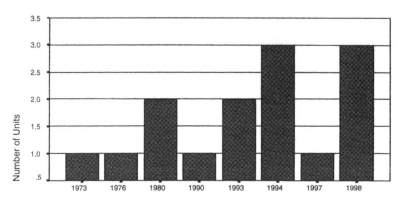

Year Proactive Practice Began

Figure 6: Proactive Use of Police Tactical Units in Canada
(Alvaro 1999 survey)

65.1% of all police services surveyed had a tactical unit, as compared to 89.4% in the United States. Furthermore, only 30.1% of the police services in smaller locales had one. This stands in contrast to the data that Kraska and Cubellis (1997) collected, where more than 65% of police services in jurisdictions between 25,000 and 50,000 in the United States had a police tactical unit.

The formation of Canadian units closely parallels the American data, with a greater number of units being formed in the mid to late seventies and again in the early 1990s. There are two differences. First, Canada had a number of years when no units were created. Second, there were more police services without a unit in the United States who were planning to establish one over the next few years. Both countries have seen the level of tactical law enforcement activities significantly rise. In the United States tactical activity had doubled by 1986, almost tripled by 1989, and quadrupled by 1995 (Kraska and Kappeler, 1997:6). Similar to the American data, Canadian unit activity also doubled by 1986, but did not triple until the early 1990s. By 1995, while the American units were being called out on average 53 times a year, the Canadian units were being deployed 76 times a year.

The Canadian data demonstrate that full-time units have already become part of everyday police operations, being called out on average every other day. The operations that these units conducted were similar to the United States. The greatest difference is that while Canadian units only spent half their time conducting

Table 2: Canadian and American Tactical Deployments

Police Tactical Unit Activities	United States	Canada
Civil disturbance	1.3%	1.6%
Terrorist incidents	.09%	0.0%
Hostage situations	3.6%	2.8%
Barricaded persons	13.4%	20.2%
High-risk warrant work/drug raids	75.9%	49.3%

Sources: Alvaro Survey (1999); Kraska and Kappeler (1997)

warrant work and drug raids the Americans spent two thirds of their time doing this work. More importantly, it is clear that these units have become more proactive than reactive.

The American data showed that 20% of the units that responded to the Kraska and Kappeler survey were proactively patrolling their jurisdictions. In Canada, the average was slightly higher: 23% of the units responding were conducting proactive patrols. However, the Canadian units tended to patrol their entire jurisdiction proactively, not just the high crime areas.

A significant difference between the American and Canadian units is the fact that military training and especially Special Forces experience in the military is highly valued and prevalent in the United States (more than 40% having had or were currently training with the military special operations personnel; Kraska and Kappeler, 1997) while in Canada this was not found to be the case. In examining the training and selection criteria of Canadian units, it was apparent that a military background was not a criterion rated highly by Canadian police tactical units. But there is a strong connection between the American and Canadian units, as many Canadian units have gone to the United Sates for training and in turn have disseminated that knowledge among other Canadian units. Therefore, the skills being taught to American police tactical units have been passed along to those Canadian units that have trained in the United States.

Conclusions

Almost all respondents in the survey felt that tactical law enforcement was a vital part of modern policing and that policing would progressively become more tactical in the future. The majority of officers also agreed that the drug epidemic (86%), violent crime (82%), and the increased use of weapons (90%) were all a significant part of the need for increases in tactical activities. There were some mixed feelings towards the drug war and several officers commented that it was not effective and was a waste of time. Another indicated that the drug war was a reason for the continued full-time status of his unit. Granted, battling drugs has caused an expansion of tactical unit activities but, as the data suggest, another activity had contributed to its expansion: dangerous/search arrest warrants, which made up 22% of all deployments that Canadian PTUs had conducted in 1997. Ninety-eight percent of the respondents agreed that tactical units should be used as often as possible in serving potentially dangerous arrest and search warrants. In addition, 73.5% agreed that a police tactical unit reduced the need for police to use force to make an arrest . All officers agreed that a tactical unit added a measure of safety for all police officers, the general public, and also the subject(s) involved. While only 78% of the respondents felt that these units did add a measure of deterrence for the criminal element within a community, it was apparent that the first objective of these units was safety of human life. Although only a few police services will create new units within the next few years, tactical commanders overwhelming felt that funding should be increased for these units (92%). There is no doubt that, in certain jurisdictions, they have become a part of mainstream policing.

Police are coming into contact with heavily armed individuals, such as street-gang members and drug dealers who have automatic military-type weapons. Police officers need to be prepared to counter criminals and to protect both themselves and the public, and therefore PTUs are welcomed by many. It has been suggested, however, that the full-time use of units could erode the public's perception of the police as being public servants and reinforce a view of police as an occupying army (Kraska, 1996:413). The wearing of fatigues, buzz hair cuts, body armour and carrying machine guns as if patrolling a war zone has the possibility of sending a negative message to the to the law-abiding citizen (Macko: 1997:34). Community relations and perceptions must be taken into account for a police force to be truly effective. A police department cannot afford to lose the confidence and cooperation of the community. Critics have said that the growing use of paramilitary style police units will threaten the idea of a civilian police force (Macko, 1997:34).

Since this area of policing is relatively new there is little empirical evidence concerning the views of the public on this subject. However, in a recent study Dennis Stevens (1999) examined the police resolutions to critical situations using tactical units. His analysis showed that tactical units enhanced the likelihood of a safer resolution to these critical incidents. The data collected for Stevens' survey showed that 96 percent of critical incidents were resolved without shots being fired once the tactical unit had arrived on the scene. Stevens found clear evidence that agencies with tactical units were able to resolve critical incidents far more safely than agencies without one. When the study examined the community's attitude towards these tactical units, however, "survey respondents revealed that they felt that police tactical units could not protect them from crime, solve crime, or prevent crime. An implication of this is that communities where highly trained paramilitary police units are operational, public confidence is lacking" (Stevens, 1999:51). Stevens concludes from his evidence that the community is actually afraid of these police tactical units and that this may be a result of the fact that they have little involvement with such units.

Policing is possibly undergoing a "quiet revolution" of democratic reforms relating to community policing. It is unclear how tactical law enforcement might play a part, or should play a part, in this new philosophy. Over 85% of the police services that maintain a tactical unit have a community policing mandate. Tactical unit members insist that their units do play a role within a community policing format. Yet, on the surface, PTUs appear the antithesis of community policing.

Eight

Women in Policing

Nancy Lewis-Horne

Introduction

Since the 1970s visible structural barriers to women's equality in policing have disappeared so that women police officers can pursue all assignments open to men within the police agency. For instance, currently women are members of the RCMP Musical Ride, and some Canadian police agencies even have female members on their tactical team. Does this mean the journey of women to achieve equality in the ranks of policing is over?

This chapter looks at the distribution of women in Canadian police agencies and considers the extent and pattern of gender segregation within the occupation of policing both in terms of types of assignments (horizontal segregation) and through the rank structure (vertical separation). Comparisons are made between national trends and trends apparent in the Ottawa Carleton Regional Police Service (OCRPS, now the Ottawa Police Service).

The Earliest Entries: 1900s to 1960

The gender division of labour and the gendered nature of police organisations are obvious in the earlier days of the modern era of policing. A review of the history reveals there was no pretense to having a gender-neutral organisation. The few women who were hired provided specialised and segregated functions consistent with the view of appropriate women's work at that time.

The history of women in the Ottawa police force, for example, can be described as following three waves, characterised by the number of women hired, their duties, and career paths. The earliest wave of women's employment in policing dates to the early 1900s. Florence Campbell was hired in 1913/1914 and retired from police duties in 1935. The hiring of Ms. Campbell in

1913 places Ottawa in a somewhat illustrious position shared by Vancouver, Edmonton, and Toronto, who record the earliest appointments of police women in Canada in 1912 and 1913. Alice Goyette was hired by the Ottawa police force in 1936. Like their counterparts in Vancouver, Edmonton, and Toronto, the early police women in Ottawa did not wear a uniform, nor were they issued firearms. In addition, Ms. Campbell and Ms. Goyette were not issued badges. Nonetheless, these early police women were provided full powers of arrest. Ms. Goyette and Ms. Campbell's responsibilities were limited to working with women and children in a protective role as victim advocates and to enforce public morality through intervening with "fallen women" (prostitutes) or women offenders. A requirement of their position was to remain unmarried.

The early experience of women hired to work in Ottawa and other Canadian police agencies parallels that of the United States and Britain. In those countries the few women hired to work in police agencies just prior to and during the First World War were hired at the insistence of women's lobby groups, charitable organisations, and political interest groups external to police agencies (Heidensohn, 1994; Moses Schulz, 1993). Women were hired in policing for a specific assignment and there was no mobility from this position. In Britain, the United States, and Canada this assignment involved performing social work and social control type functions with women and children. Consequently, the occasional hiring of a few women to perform gender-specific assignments did not threaten the male ethos of policing. Policing remained a male occupation and no male police officer had to work with or be supervised by a woman.

Post-War Entries: 1945 to 1970

The second wave in the employment of women in policing spanned the post-war period. Changes in the employment experience of women in policing during this period mirrored changes occurring in the remainder of society as a result of the war effort. Women's roles in society changed during the war years including the acceptance and even encouragement of women to enter the paid labour market and the armed services. Women worked on the factory floor and they managed the paperwork and support services that drove the military effort. Consequently, it was no longer unheard of for a woman to wear a uniform or to pursue paid employment. In addition the growth in police recruitment following the war was fuelled by the hiring of returned veterans — men who were familiar with the work of women in the military.

The employment of Edna Harry with the Ottawa police force in 1946 fits this pattern. As with women hired by police agencies throughout Canada, the United States, and Britain, Edna Harry was issued a uniform. However, similar to her predecessors, Campbell and Goyette, her duties were restricted to intervening with women and children, victims and offenders. Unlike her American colleagues she was not issued a firearm. Edna Harry remained a police woman working in the detective office until retirement.

The employment of women with the Ottawa Police Force during this period has an interesting and somewhat unique twist. Although Edna Harry's duties were consistent with the gender-specific duties of the earlier wave of police women, Ottawa hired some women to perform duties which had previously been assigned to male police officers. As with their colleagues in the United States, women were assigned to a separate women's bureau. In the case of Ottawa this was officially referred to as the Women's Auxiliary and administratively referred to as the Women's Division. It should be noted the title of Women's Auxiliary was not supported by the women; instead, the women wished to be referred to as police women but the administration refused.

With the exception of Ms. Harry, the work performed by women of the Women's Division with the Ottawa Police was different from the tasks assigned the first wave of police women. But as was characteristic of the earlier wave, their duties were very limited as was their career progression. In addition, women hired during this second wave were structurally and organisationally separated from the "real work of policing," which the men performed. The assignment of new tasks for the women was driven by changes occurring in the city of Ottawa in the 1960s, as well as the changing needs of its police force. Following the Second World War, the federal public service expanded, creating problems of traffic congestion in Ottawa, especially in the area around government buildings. To deal with this, those in the Women's Division were assigned to traffic duty, enforcing the Highway Traffic Act and city by-laws, issuing parking tickets and directing traffic.

In her review of the history of women employed with the Ottawa police, Sergeant Cori Slaughter (2000) argues that women were assigned to new tasks such as parking enforcement because these were tasks policemen did not wish to pursue. This point is revealed in a statement, as cited by Slaughter, from former Chief of Police Axcell describing the efficiencies of hiring women:

A trained police officer is wasted on parking enforcement when there are so many other ways his training
and experience could be applied. Furthermore, as these
men are subjected to continual abuse, the work is distasteful to them, so much so that several men have re-
signed rather than continue with it ...

Employment of these women would release 25 trained
men for other more important duties. (Slaughter, 2000)

Consequently the assignment of these tasks to women increased
the employment of women in policing while at the same time rel-
egating women to segregated and "ghettoised" assignments not
highly valued in the police organisation.

Members of the Women's Division were not welcomed with
open arms by their male co-workers. Although the men did not
enjoy the duties of parking enforcement they resented the loss of
the one perk this entailed: the day shifts involved. Traffic enforcement was a nine-to-five job, Monday to Friday. Assigning traffic
enforcement solely to the Women's Division resulted in fewer day
shifts for male police officers. Consequently the women did not
get much assistance or support from their male co-workers.

Influenced by the experience of women serving in the armed
forces during the Second World War, women in the second wave
were issued a uniform. However, the uniform reflected gender-
appropriate images and differentiated the women from the men.
Women's uniforms included white skirts for walking and trousers
for riding a scooter. Even on very cold winter days, Ottawa's police
women wore skirts. They were issued a shoulder bag to complete
and complement the uniform.

During this period, 1945 to 1970, the number of women
hired by the Ottawa Police Force and other police agencies in North
America and Britain increased substantially. For instance, on May
13, 1960, 21 women graduated from recruit training and went to
work for the Ottawa Police Force. During the 1960s approximately
50 women were hired to work with the Ottawa Police Force. These
women had the same six weeks of training as male officers and
had the same powers of arrest. However, they were still not issued
firearms.

There was a large turnover in the Women's Division as the
earlier job requirement shared by the first wave of police women
continued: police women had to remain single with no child de-
pendents. Thus, if a woman became pregnant or wished to marry,
she had to resign. Women also left because there were no other

101

career opportunities for them in the police force. Women in Ottawa left to take jobs outside of policing, often with the federal public service.

Increased hiring of women in the Ottawa Police Force came to an abrupt end in the 1970s. Instead, at this time the police force began a cadet program for males between the ages of 18 and 21. These young cadets assumed many of the responsibilities Women's Division officers had previously performed. Unlike the women's career progression, young male cadets at 21 years of age entered recruit training as full constables with all powers of a sworn officer.

Of the approximately 50 women hired as part of the Women's Division during the 1960s seven remained with the police service in 1973. That year, the Ontario Police Commission abolished Women's Divisions throughout the province. All women employed in Women's Divisions were amalgamated into the general policing ranks and were provided the same rate of pay, benefits and seniority as the men. Prior to this public announcement by the Ontario Police Commission, members of the Women's Division of the Ottawa Police Force were solicited by then Chief of Police Seguin to become civilian employees and give up their status and powers as a sworn police officer. Six of the remaining seven women did undergo recruit training, were issued firearms, standard issue uniforms and provided peace officer status. However, the practice of segregated assignment and duties did not change, as these women were assigned paperwork duties, not general patrol duties.

Both the first and second waves of police women experienced a narrowly defined gender division of labour. Even though the pattern of the tasks and assignments differed between the groups they all performed specific duties defined as "women's work". Whether the women performed social work functions with women and children as victims or offenders, paper work, or "meter maid" duties, these areas of responsibility were seen as more appropriate for women's abilities and skills and were accorded less organisational reward and value. In addition to the narrowly defined gender division of labour, there were few employment growth opportunities for women in policing. Few women were hired and even fewer stayed with the job until retirement or financial independence allowed them to resign.

A distinguishing feature of these earlier periods of employment for women in policing is that there was no pretense to equality of opportunity for women or that the police organisation was anything more than a male world. Women were not provided equal pay to that of their male co-workers and their association was terminated once they became the dependent of a husband. It is not until the contemporary period in women's employment in policing that there is any pretense to gender neutrality or gender equality.

Current Entry: 1970 to the present

The third wave of women in policing begins in the mid-1970s and is characterised by increased hiring, and the integration and normalisation of duties for women. It is important to acknowledge the significant role governments in Canada and the United States played in extending gender equality rights and the role played by the judiciary and administrative law tribunals in enforcing equity rights.

Canadian women used recently implemented human rights legislation to gain access to Canadian police agencies and to equalise the playing field with males. For instance, following the Ontario Police Commissions ruling to disband Women's Divisions in 1973, the Ottawa Police Force did not hire additional women as sworn peace officers until the fall of 1979. In 1979 the Ottawa Police Force unsuccessfully defended itself to the Ontario Human Rights Commission Board of Inquiry against a complaint by Ann Colfer, who did not meet the physical height and weight requirement (5'10" and 160 lbs.) for successful applicants. According to Colfer, a sociology graduate, her application to the Ottawa Police Force was not seriously considered. She informed a reporter for the *Globe and Mail* (Bell, 1977) that "most questions at both interviews [with the Ottawa Police Force] centred around her sex and marital status and little attention was paid to her experience as a voluntary probation officer or abilities and career plans." The Ottawa Police Force was ordered by the Ontario Human Rights Commission to process Miss Colfer's application ahead of others and to amend its hiring standard to accommodate women. Taken together, judicial, quasi-judicial, and legislative support for gender equality allowed women to pursue employment in policing in increased numbers and on terms equal to males.

In contrast to the Ottawa Police Force's hiring policies of the 1970s, the RCMP graduated its first troop (Troop 17) of 32 women on March 3, 1975. These women were the first in RCMP history to "hold the rank of constable and the title of regular member in the RCMP" (Serry, 1995:13). Other major municipal police agencies recruited women and assigned them to general patrol duties during the 1970s. For example, the first time women were assigned to general patrol duties with the Vancouver Police Department was in 1973; by 1977, sworn female peace officers comprised approximately 5 percent of the department (Linden, 1984:6).

The elimination of height and weight standards that discriminated against women and were proven not to be a bona fide occupational qualification allowed women to gain access to careers in police work. Women also fought other policies that served to discriminate against their full participation in police work and restrict their ability to achieve their career ambitions. For instance, two Ontario police women fought their employer for the right to maintain their employment status while pregnant. In one case a Divisional Court Justice ruled a police woman with the Fort Frances Police Force had been "directly" discriminated against, when her employer refused to provide her part-time clerical duties during her pregnancy (Allard, 1989:14). Similarly, in the case of a woman employed with the Ottawa Police Force, once her pregnancy was made public, police administrators attempted to have her suspended without pay. Both police agencies believed the women should suspend their employment at least temporarily and apply for maternity benefits from the government. Judicial decision-making in the earlier case of the Fort Francis police woman determined that the treatment afforded male police officers who experienced health-related issues was different as the police agency provided these officers the opportunity to perform part-time clerical duties until they returned to full duties. The case of the Ottawa police woman did not go to trial. Instead, the Mayor of Ottawa advocated for continued employment in the form of light duties for her and the police commission instructed the police chief to assign the police woman to the property room instead of suspending her duties entirely. The current practice of Canadian police agencies is to assign pregnant police women to "light duties". Some police agencies even provide uniforms to accommodate pregnant police women's altered form.

The third wave of women employed in policing have fought for and won the opportunity to work in all assignments within their occupation; for instance, women were assigned to the RCMP Musical Ride beginning in 1981. A few women have won coveted positions in tactical teams: as members of police agencies including the RCMP riot squad, women were on the security line during the Conference of the Americas held in Quebec City in April 2001. A few women have made their way through the rank structure to gain top positions in a limited number of Canadian police agencies including Gwen Boniface, Commissioner of the Ontario Provincial

Police; Christine Silverberg, retired as Chief of Police for the Calgary Police Service; Lenna Bradburn, retired as Chief of the Guelph Police Service, and currently Director of Investigations and Complaints Resolution for the office of Ombudsman in the province of Ontario. A few women are also well placed in senior management positions within the RCMP, including Deputy Commissioner Beverly Busson and Chief Superintendents Lynn Twardosky, Barbara George, and Gessie Clement.

This third wave of police women have fought other battles to achieve equality of opportunity within Canadian police agencies including extended maternity rights and benefits, parental leave, and comfortable and serviceable uniforms. And they continue to fight for a work environment respectful of their femininity.

Statistical Distribution of Women in Policing

The percentage of women comprising sworn peace officer status has increased during the past 30 years. Whether we consider the percentage increase or the growth in real numbers of women in policing, the increase of women in policing is dramatic. In the 33 years from 1965 to 1998, the representation of women in policing has grown from 0.6% of police officers to 12.2%; that is, from 190 to 6,686 women.

However, two limitations to the apparent good news associated with the statistical distribution must be noted. First, depending on whether you view the bottle as half empty or half full, 12.2% of sworn officer strength after 30 years of women in policing may be considered as good news — or evidence of an unfulfilled promise. While women comprise approximately 51% of all communities in Canada, they do not represent 51% of those with the power to enforce the law in our communities. Even if we compare the percentage of women participating in the paid labour force and actively seeking employment with the percentage of women employed in policing there is a noticeable gap. A reasonable comparison would examine the employment level of those aged 25 to 54 years, as this age range most closely resembles those targetted for recruitment and currently serving police officers. The employment level for women increases to between 71-74% if we narrow the age range from 25 to 54 years (Statistics Canada, 2000). Consequently, even though almost 3 out of 4 women in this age range participate in the paid labour force, few of these women are employed as police officers across the country.

Second, the statistical distribution of women in policing was based on aggregate figures representing an average of all police women across the country. Thus, the percentage of women working in police agencies across the country varies: some police agencies have more than the average of 12.9% women (1999 rates), while others included considerably fewer. For instance, 15.29% of women sworn officers in Ottawa-Carleton (OCRPS) compares favourably with the national average of 12.9% and the provincial Ontario average of 13.6% (CCJS, 1999:12). However, the percentage of women police officers in OCRPS was lower than the British Columbia average of 16.5%. The percentage of women police officers in OCRPS did exceed that in the remaining provinces and territories. Provincial and territorial averages record a range of women police officers between 7.2% (Nunavut) and 16.5% (B.C.).

Looking at recruitment figures confirms the important relationship between government policy and hiring practices. During the years 1991, 1994, and 1995, while the equity provisions contained in Ontario's Police Services Act were in effect, the three police agencies (prior to amalgamation) for Ottawa, Nepean, and Gloucester, hired more female recruits than male recruits (refer to Table 1, later in this chapter). During the period 1990–1995, the percentage of women hired as recruits range from a high of 56.68% in 1991 to a low of almost 29% in 1993. In contrast, during the next 5 years (beginning in 1996 with the repeal of the equity provisions in the Police Services Act initiated by Premier Harris), the percentage of women hired as recruits ranged from a high of almost 25% in 1999 to a low of less than 12% in 1996. Consequently, the highest percentage of women recruited to the Ottawa Carleton Regional Police Service after repeal of the legislated equity provisions (24.42% in 1997) was lower than the lowest percentage of women recruited when the legislated equity provisions directed hiring policy (40% in 1990 and 1992 respectively).

In addition to examining the national distribution of women in policing, some greater detail as to their employment, such as job assignment, is revealing. Research found women employed as police officers with OCRPS were not evenly distributed throughout the police organisation in either horizontal assignment pattern or vertical promotion. Women are over-represented in some assignments, and especialy in general patrol duties (referred to as "district policing" by the OCRPS). In fact, 78 percent of all police women at the rank of constable with the OCRPS are assigned to patrol duties, while only 51 percent of all police men of the same rank are assigned to the same task. Further refined, one in four general patrol constables are women, yet women account for only

15% of police officer strength, supporting the point that women are over-represented in general patrol duties. This imbalance is consistent with interview data suggesting that women value patrol work and expect it will be a continual element in their policing careers. Consequently, women may be fostering this situation, thereby contributing to the gender division of labour within the OCRPS.

Although the existence of a gender division of labour within OCRPS is consistent with international research examining women in policing (e.g., Heidensohn, 1994; Jonas, 1986), the OCRPS pattern of a feminising trend in patrol work is somewhat unique. Research from other countries shows different patterns of women's work in policing. For instance, research in Britain and the United States reveals that police-women are becoming re-ghettoised into the traditional functions of sexual- and child-abuse investigations, domestic violence units, school liaison units etc. Research from Britain reveals that police women are kept out of special units such as dog handling, mounted branch and fire arms duties.

Similar to the experience of police women in the first and second waves, today's police women are more likely to be working in assignments less valued by the organisation and in jobs male officers do not wish to pursue. Recent research by Miller (1999) reveals that male officers are more likely than their female counterparts to move into assignments with improved organisational rewards such as overtime compensation and increased opportunity for promotion. As male officers moved into these positions Miller found female officers were less likely to hold these positions. Similarly, examination of OCRPS revealed that assignments highly valued in the organisation are those in which women are under-represented (Miller, 1999). Examples of such assignments include investigative units such as Criminal Investigations Division (CID) and operational specialty units (canine, tactical team). A male police constabl eis twice as likely to achieve a position in CID as is a female. What is more, as we focus the level of analysis more narrowly to examine specific job tasks and assignments within CID, the gendered division of labour becomes increasingly obvious. Of the 21 investigative units comprising CID, 16 do not have a woman investigator working within the unit. Investigative units with the highest proportion of women are those involved in sexual assault, child abuse, spousal assault, and the regional drug squads. As a result, women are less likely to work in the more prestigious CID assignments than their male co-workers and those few women who manage to gain a CID assignment are found in only one quarter of all CID units.

Gender segregation of the OCRPS labour force was evident vertically as well as horizontally. Of particular note is the fact that women are under-represented in the higher ranks in assignments in which they predominate as constables. For example, women are less likely than men to be supervisors in general patrol policing or to serve as lead investigators or supervisors in sexual assault, child abuse, or drug investigation units. Analysis reveals that women first line supervisors are more likely to be employed in an area involving either investigative or support services such as professional development and court liaison, than in one involving personnel supervision. Thus, few men in policing have the experience of working directly for a woman. At the rank of constable, 75 percent are men, whereas 91 percent are women. As one moves up the rank structure, the under-representation of women becomes increasingly obvious.

The vertical segregation evident in the OCRPS is consistent with trends noted in other American and Canadian studies. They also indicate that women have made some strides in obtaining middle management positions, but are vastly under represented in senior management positions. Also, because of their small numbers within police agencies, women have little impact on major decision making, and have minimal authority over male employees within the organisation.

Table 1: Percentage of female police officers within the ranks

	Constable	Non-commissioned (first- and second-line supervisor)	Senior officer (Inspector and above)
American Statistics[a]	14.7%	9.6%	7.5%
Canadian Statistics[b]	16.2%	4.7%	2.8%

[a]Feminist Majority Foundation (1999); [b]CCJS (1999).

Two sources of information — an assessment of the status of women in policing in 1998 by the Feminist Majority Foundation (1999) and an evaluation of police resources in 1999 by Statistics Canada (CCJS, 1999) — quantify the hierarchical division of labour within American and Canadian police agencies. The data in Table 1 confirm that police management continues to be a gendered occupation. Analysis reveals that women are most under-represented in top senior officer positions followed by supervisory positions.

Conclusions

The purpose of this chapter was to demonstrate the existence of a gender division of labour in policing: although 90 years have passed since women were first employed as police officers, gender continues to matter in the occupation of policing, structuring women's opportunities within the police agency. Although police organisations appear to advocate gender neutrality and equality, the existence of a gender-segregated division of labour means that gender equality has not been achieved.

In some obvious respects women have come a long way—women now comprise more than token status in police organisations. Women on patrol can meet other women on patrol. It is no longer novel to observe a woman performing police duties in the community. Many in the occupation of policing reproduce the discourse presenting the police organisation and occupation as gender-neutral and can point to individual women who have successfully achieved high rank in various Canadian police organisations.

However, closer examination demonstrates the existence of a gender division of labour, with women relegated to those positions of lesser value within the police organisation. Police organisations do not provide equality of opportunity for women employees, nor do they practice gender neutrality. If they did, a structural analysis of police organisations would not find feminising trends evident in those assignments least valued in policing, and prestige assignments and physical spaces reproducing the male ethos of policing (Lewis-Horne, 2001).

Nine

Police Work and Marriage

Caryn Moulton

Introduction

The goal of this chapter is to provide an overview of policing issues that affect the marital relationships of police officers, focussing on organisational pressures, police peer pressures, job-related attitudes and behaviours, ineffective communication and coping behaviours, and social and interpersonal problems.

There has been much controversy over the divorce rates within police departments (e.g., Kroes, Margolis, and Hurrell, 1974; Terry, 1981; Watson and Sterling, 1969) and it is apparent that the police profession has a profound effect on the police marriage (e.g., Maynard and Maynard, 1982; Reiser, 1978). Elements of police work may cause unique stresses and problems within marriages that are not found in the "normal" population. Stress in the lives of police officers in turn affects their health, job performances, and personal and family lives (e.g., Kroes, et al., 1974).

The quality of marital and family relationships can influence a police officer's quality of work while at his/her job (Burke, 1988; Maynard, Maynard, McCubbin, and Shao, 1980; Staines and Pleck, 1983; Piotrowski, 1979); for example, negative family interactions may affect their judgment and concentration while on duty. Because police officers are often involved in situations that demand sound judgment it is imperative that stresses be understood and addressed, to minimise interference in job performance, as well as maintaining a balanced home life.

Organisational Pressures

Organisational pressures can be described as the expectations for police officers' work commitment, working hours, and promotional opportunities. Expectations for police officers to fully commit to their career often begins with the recruit training process, in which new police officers are expected to devote most of their time to their police service. In Canada, recruits are taken away from family commitments and responsibilities anywhere from 12 weeks (Ontario Police College) to 6 months (RCMP college), where they are involved in stressful and demanding training procedures. Most of these colleges do not provide child care or housing where families can remain intact while the new officer attends the college.

Although the expectation for total commitment may begin at the early stages of recruit training, it does not end there. Arahan (1984) believes that the commitment to police work is the result of an expectation to identify with, and be loyal to, fellow officers. Many police officers are made to feel that the requirements of the job should take precedence over any other commitment, including their family. Many families adjust by simply accepting second priority to the officer's career. However, for other families it remains a constant source of resentment and conflict. Along with the department's expectations of commitment, police officers are often expected to work over-time and in shift rotations. The officer's family is often forced to adjust its own schedules to conform to the shift or over-time requirements; the long hours of separation can cause domestic problems (Alexander and Walker, 1996; Hattery and Merrill, 1997; Nicholas, 1973).

Nicoletti and Spooner (1994) suggest that the family is affected by shift work because they are forced to rotate and adjust their lives to the officer's work requirements. Stenmark, et al. (1982) also examined the impact that shift work has on the police officer's family. Police spouses (wives) were divided into two groups — "satisfied" or "dissatisfied" with their husbands' career. Dissatisfied wives (that is, women who thought their lives would be better if they were not a member of a police family) reported higher levels of concern about their husbands' working hours and the effect on meal planning and social activities, when compared to satisfied wives.

Maynard and Maynard (1982) also found irregular working hours caused increased levels of stress for some police officers' spouses. Police wives from a large metropolitan police force were asked what aspects of their husband's career negatively affected their family. The wives reported irregular working hours (among others) to be stressful because it prevented them from fully pursuing their own careers. Sacrifices often had to be made in their own careers, as their working hours would have been in conflict with their husbands'.

Police: Selected Issues

In contrast, a study conducted by Alexander (1994) examined the stress of shift work on a large sample of police wives. Although shift work, long hours, dangerous duties, and inability to change roles when returning home, were of some concern, half of the police wives felt that these stresses were only slightly harmful to the marital relationship, and only a very small number felt they were extremely harmful. The majority of the wives did not feel these stresses were harmful to their own health, their family, or their social life. This empirical study suggests that shift work may not increase stress levels within relationships.

Only a small percentage of police wives in these studies were concerned about the negative impact that shift work had upon their lives. Certain types of police spouses may not find shift work to negatively impact on the marriage. For example, partners who work or who have a number of social contacts may not find shift work to be as disruptive to the family. On the other hand, this suggests that it may be specific types of marriages (e.g., troubled marriages) that are most affected by shift work. For example, spouses who have less social support, who wait for their spouses to return, may find adjusting to shift work and over-time demands difficult.

Total commitment to the force, shift work, and over-time may *physically* remove the officer from the family; however, lack of promotional opportunities and lack of support within the department may *emotionally* remove the officer from the family (Burke, 1988). If a police officer is depressed, discouraged, resentful, angry, or frustrated with the job or superiors, it is likely that this anger will be brought home. Research conducted by Hart, Wearing, and Headey (1995) provides empirical support for the link between lack of promotional opportunities and stress levels of police officers. Police officers' levels of psychological well-being were measured and then compared to other occupational groups. The positive and negative work experiences that contribute to their psychological well-being were also measured. Results indicated that organisational pressures (e.g., promotions and lack of support) were more influential in determining officers' overall level of psychological well-being than were operational pressures (e.g., criminals or victims).

Does lack of support and promotional opportunity also affect other members of the family? Grossman (1994) suggests that families hope for promotional opportunities as much as the officer. More money leads to to more financial security, as success in today's society is often measured by power, occupational prestige, and money. Stenmark, et al. (1982) asked police wives to rate various stresses that they may face: lack of support and promotional possibilities was rated as the most stressful element of their husband's career. Most believed police promotional systems were unfair and were discouraged about their husband's future. Additionally, the police officer often became depressed, angry, and resentful, which forced the spouse to not only cope with her own disappointment but also with the officer's sense of hopelessness.

Maynard and Maynard (1982) also examined the association between lack of promotional opportunities and satisfaction of police wives. Findings revealed that a lack of promotional opportunities and political attitudes of the department discouraged the wives, upset the husband (i.e., officer), and affected family life. The officers often carried their frustrations home, targetting the family with displaced anger. The wives also felt that it was their responsibility to understand job-related difficulties and to discuss the problems with their husbands. The wives reported that it was difficult to see their husbands struggling with decisions that were correct and proper, but not politically best for the department.

Police Peer Pressures

Although lack of promotional opportunities and lack of support may create some animosity among fellow officers and towards administration, police officers remain a tightly knit group of individuals. These individuals form a type of social group or a mini-society of their own. Recently, many text books and papers have referred to this concept as the "police subculture" (Borum and Philpot, 1993; Bradstreet, 1994; Cox, 1996). The subculture is said to consist of informal rules and regulations, passed on from generation to generation (Cox, 1996). Sparrow, Moore, and Kennedy (1990) suggest the following set of "truths" are found in most police forces: (1) only fellow officers can be trusted and truly understand the nature of police work, (2) loyalty to fellow police officers should be top priority, and (3) the public is generally unsupportive of and unreasonable about police officers.

These "truths" may be part of the socialisation that influences the police officer from the very beginning of the training process (Roberg and Kuykendall, 1993). For example, recruits are removed from their usual residence and transferred to training facilities in which many months are spent learning the specific rules of law enforcement. It is here that the recruits begin to understand the "codes" of policing. Away from the general public and even their own family and support systems, recruits are often forced to interact solely with other officers and other police personnel. Once the initial stage of training is complete, the new recruits then learn "real" policing from senior officers. The negative attitudes that senior officers may have towards the rest of society are often displayed and reinforced to the new recruits, and eventually the new recruits adopt these as their own. When the norms and standards within the police subculture become their own, they may isolate themselves from the rest of society — physically, emotionally, and mentally. Thus, the new recruits are likely to become even more dependent on fellow officers and other police personnel for support, safety, personal needs, and attention. The spouse, along with other family members and close friends, may be alienated and left on the periphery of the police officer's life.

Borum and Philpot (1993) agree with this police subculture description and argue that many elements of this special "society" will have a negative impact upon the family. The strong bond among police officers is partly the result of the mistrust they have for others. Many police officers believe that only other officers can understand the complexities of their job, and thus they tend to associate only amongst themselves. This promotes trust only among other members and may interfere with personal relationships outside the police profession.

As a result of a predominantly male profession, police departments resemble a type of fraternity where stereotypic masculine values and attitudes are enforced (Borum and Philpot, 1993). Characteristics such as control, dominance, and authority are reinforced by both the demands of the job and fellow officers. Additionally, activities such as drinking and sexual behaviour may be held in high regard within the police profession. Such characteristics, reinforced at work, are contrary to those that are necessary to maintain intimate relationships. Thus, it seems that socialisation processes that occur within the police department undermine marital and familial relationships.

Identifying with other officers

Police officers associate primarily with one another for a variety of reasons. Reiser (1978) suggests that new recruits have a strong need to bolster their ego and exert their new-found authority. Thus, the new police officer may spend time bonding with other officers, often at the expense of time spent with his/her spouse. The spouse may eventually begin to feel lonely, neglected, and even resentful.

Arahan (1984) suggests that the need to establish the male identity and to bond with fellow officers may cause the officer to exaggerate characteristics associated with maleness (i.e., strength, aggressiveness) and deny any of the characteristics associated with femininity (i.e., emotions such as gentleness, tenderness, fear). However, the officer who exerts this type of masculine behaviour will often find him/herself in conflict at home. Portraying both a tough cop and a loving and supportive husband/wife is hard to accomplish. Thus, if the officer is unable to fulfill the role of spouse, he/she may eventually withdraw and seek emotional support elsewhere.

Sexual behaviours

Because the police profession is still very much predominantly male, many police officers feel the need to exert their masculinity and prove themselves to other fellow officers (Borum and Philpot, 1993). A common stereotype held about police officers is their tendency to engage in extramarital affairs. Neiderhoffer and Niederhoffer (1978) argue that the number of affairs police officers engage in are often exaggerated, leading to rumours and stereotypes within and about the police department. No empirical study has compared the rate of extramarital affairs in the police forces to that in the normal population.

However, Reiser (1973) suggests that fraternity-type attitudes often include the need to exhibit masculine behaviour. Thus, officers may engage in extramarital affairs to prove their masculinity, becoming preoccupied with proving himself to his fellow officers.

Territo and Vetter (1981) discuss infidelity as a problem for both the officer and the officer's spouse. Couples with each spouse working the oppositite shift encounter such basic problems as scheduling their sex lives. This can lead to frustration and hostility towards one another and can result in one or both partners seeking sexual partners elsewhere.

Lack of respect for marriage

With the high emphasis placed on male bonding and the pressures to exert masculine behaviours (e.g., sexual encounters), there are some who believe that the police, as an organisation, do not respect the "sanctity" of marriage (e.g., Maynard and Maynard, 1982; Reiser, 1973). However, despite such views, the empirical studies that have examined the attitudes of police officers towards marriage are scarce. A study conducted by Maynard and Maynard

(1982) examined concerns police wives had about peer and departmental pressures against marriage and family. Over half of the wives in the study indicated that they were of the impression that police officers in general did not think marriage and family to be important and that an anti-marriage attitude existed within their husbands' departments. It appears as though the socialisation processes within police departments are anti-marriage in that many of the expectations and pressures to conform and prove oneself are antithetical to marriages.

Job-Related Attitudes and Behaviours

There are several types of attitudes (beside anti-family ones) that exist within the police department: suspicion, overprotectiveness, jealousy, control, and authoritarianism are common (Nordlicht, 1979) in police officers.They are not conducive to a stable, healthy marriage.

Suspiciousness and overprotectiveness

Most people with whom the police officer comes into contact are offenders of various types. Daily interactions among criminals, along with gruesome accident scenes and domestic violence, force the officer to look at life in a grim way (Stratton, 1975). Eventually, this constant bombardment of "negative" life events influences the officer's own perception of the quality of life, and may influence the officer's attitudes towards certain situations and people. The officer may view all others as a potential threat and may want to protect the family from any harm: physically, emotionally, and mentally. Stratton (1975) believes that the trauma and degradation that an officer observes each day causes them to become overly protective of their own family. The officer may feel the responsibility to protect them from seeing or learning about the tragic aspects of life that they themselves witness every day. The police officer may also become suspicious and overly concerned about who their spouse is with, where they are, and what they are doing. While the officer may be genuinely concerned for their spouse's safety, the spouse may perceive it as intrusive and may resent the lack of trust and confidence that the officer has in their judgment.

Bradstreet (1994) also suggests that it is the *kind* of work that police officers encounter that often encourages these types of attitudes to surface. Officers begin to see everyone as a potential liar, cheat, or scam artist. Because of their unique profession and the duties that they are required to fulfill, Bradstreet suggests that officers develop an "us vs. them" attitude. The officers do not feel that anyone, other than a fellow officer, understands what it is like to be a police officer. Thus, officers trust very few outside of the organisation, perhaps even their own spouses.

Arahan (1984) argues that negativity and cynicism is common among police officers because of their constant exposure to danger and violence. Police officers may become chronically anxious about their spouses' safety and integrity, and may try to impose serious restrictions on the family, which inevitably causes conflict within it.

Control

Within the police subculture there is a need to feel in control and to protect (Bradstreet, 1994). New officers are specially trained to take control of situations, of their emotions, and of other people — it is imperative for their survival. This need to take complete control can impede a healthy relationship, as it is counterproductive to intimacy (Reiser, 1978; Stratton, 1975). An officer who is in control at work may find it difficult to give up this authority when returning home. Trying to control one's spouse and their life may cause feelings of resentment and rebellion.

Because police organisations are still paramilitary in their structure, there is a clear chain of command where orders are passed down and obeyed quickly. Successful officers develop a quick ability to take and make orders while on duty. These "take-charge" behaviours that help the officer on the street are not helpful in the home. Spouses are not as subservient as street offenders, who see the officer as an authority figure to fear. When officers are not able to control situations at home they may try and deal with it by becoming even more controlling and authoritarian. Spouses may end up lying, sneaking, and rebelling against their officer spouse, as resenting the mistrust and controlling behaviour.

Additionally, officers who are controlling generally do not engage in effective communication skills (Bradstreet, 1994), which is crucial within a marriage. Officers who do not listen to, or respond to, their spouse's needs, thoughts, or concerns may contribute to problems within the marriage. The spouse may begin to feel frustrated and resentful and may look for comfort and understanding elsewhere.

Ineffective Communication and Coping Behaviours

Being in control of situations and other people's lives often helps police officers to cope with the problems they face daily. Police officers may also use other types of coping behaviours to help them function "normally" in spite of the nature of their work. Unfortunately, many of these, like attitudes, are contrary to the success of a marital relationship. Behaviours such as ineffective communication, emotional detachment, and alcohol have all been linked to marital conflict.

Ineffective communication

Ineffective communication between couples can lead to marital breakdown. Communication breakdown in police marriages is often due to reasons different from those found in non-police marriages. There are a number of reasons why a police officer may choose not to talk to their spouse about problems at work, problems at home, and their feelings in general. These include the need to protect their spouse, a perceived incompetency of that spouse, confidentiality, and emotional exhaustion.

Stratton (1975) suggests that police officers refrain from talking to their spouses about the job because of the gruesome details that are involved in their work. The officer may feel that the details of work will cause problems, and that he/she may find it difficult to cope with the things the officer is required to do, see, and experience. Police officers may also be afraid to show their spouses that they are troubled by certain experiences, as this may indicate weakness and incompetence.

Reiser (1978) reports that many police officers begin to think of their spouses as incompetent and boring. While some spouses may be doing "boring" jobs, the police officer is out in the community, being challenged and meeting new and interesting people. The officer may feel that his/her spouse is not capable of understanding the complexities of their work, and thus do not attempt to involve the spouse in any concerns or problems they may be having. Police officers may discuss their problems with fellow officers whom they feel are better suited to understanding them. Thus, the more officers turn to one another for emotional support, the greater the emotional distance created between the officer and their spouse. With such a negative perception of the spouses' competencies and lack of respect for their role in the relationship, police officers may begin to believe that their problems are the most important, and thus may also fail to meet the emotional needs of their partner.

It is also possible that police officers do not feel comfortable talking with their spouses about work-related matters because of confidentiality issues (Arahan, 1984). Officers may feel they are betraying this confidentiality by telling *anyone* about the aspects of the police investigations. For example, the Police Services Act of Ontario instruct officers to keep what they see, hear, or learn, in confidence unless the performance of duty or legal provision requires otherwise (Police Services Act, Code of Conduct, Ontario Reg. 927). As well, many investigations require officers to remain silent so that cases are not contaminated through leakage of information to the public. Thus, police officers are somewhat forced to talk only among themselves and exclude their spouses from their conversations.

With everything that they see and do, it is also very likely that police officers are emotionally exhausted at the end of the day (Territo and Veter, 1981). Police officers are constantly bombarded by negative problems that they are required to solve, which may lead to frustration and psychological exhaustion. At the end of the shift, the officer's tolerance level may be very low, and any problems at home may provoke overwhelming emotions, and possibly anger. The officer may become infuriated at the smallest and simplest transgression, and may be in no state to discuss problems related to work or family. This displaced anger and ignorance of family problems will leave the majority of the parental responsibilities to the spouse.

Bradstreet (1994) believes that effective police work requires the police officer to be objective. When emotions are involved officers may become personally invested in situations and may be distracted from solving the problems at hand. Displaying any type of weakness such as crying or sadness is often described by veteran officers as "losing it". Officers deal with the trauma of their work by developing an outer shell and acting tough and indifferent to human suffering (Nordlicht, 1979). Territo and Vetter (1981) suggest that most police officers find it necessary to suppress their feelings in order to function adequately on the job to avoid deep personal involvement in the upsetting and traumatic experiences that they are often forced to deal with. This suppression also allows officers to perform unpleasant and distasteful but necessary tasks without displaying any emotion. Officers are trained to control their emotions while on the job, and thus often learn how to deny feelings of anger, disgust, and sadness.

At home, these same coping behaviours are detrimental to the marital relationship. The officers actively avoid discussing issues with spouses where conflict or tension may arise, and as a result these issues are left unresolved. This may create emotional distance between the marriage partners, as the spouse may come to perceive the officer as a robot who is no longer capable of being an intimate partner. Lack of emotions and the inability to express feelings and thoughts may ultimately lead to communication breakdown and marital dissolution. Spouses may will want to share their feelings and thoughts, but may be unable to get through the officer's stoicism (Reiser, 1978). The couple may stop communicating and other areas of the marriage may begin to deteriorate.

In sum, regardless of the reason for communication breakdown, spouses are left out of a very large and important part of police officers' lives. Additionally, they themselves are deprived of an emotionally supportive partner.

Alcoholism

Along with emotional suppression, officers may deal with the grim details of work by escaping reality. Alcohol has often been used as a way in which police officers deal with job-related stresses (Beehr, Johnson, and Nieva, 1995; Nordlicht, 1979). Officers may abuse alcohol because it is widely accepted by society as a stress reducer and is an integral part of social interaction (Borum and Philpot, 1993). Excessive drinking is at times encouraged as a way to unwind after a hard shift or stressful incident.

Reiser (1978) contends that social drinking is accepted and even highly valued as a tension reducer and a way to unwind within the department. However, police administrators are also concerned about spiraling effects: officers who show signs of alcohol-related problems may jeopardise career advancements. Contradictory messages from the organisation can cause confusion for the officer who feels encouraged to have a few drinks, but is punished if it goes beyond that which the administration deems reasonable.

Stratton (1975) suggests that drinking often occurs after the late shift where fellow officers are available to talk but spouses and families are not. Police officers may be able to let their guard down after a few drinks and admit weaknesses or failings under these more accepting circumstances, where a protective image is unnecessary. Stratton also links excessive drinking to the masculine image of strength and power that is promoted within the department. With these attitudes, officers can maintain their "he-man" image, and at the same time voice their concerns.

Although some officers may employ ineffective coping strategies (i.e., drinking, emotional suppression), lack of empirical support prevents generalisation to *all* police couples. In fact, Maynard and Maynard (1982) and Cherry and Lester (1979) examined the coping techniques of police officers and their families, and found that spending time with family and planning family activities were the preferred coping techniques, by both the police officer and the family. Alcohol was rated as the least effective coping behaviour.

Social and Interpersonal Issues

The social lives of police families are also affected by the police profession. Police families are often isolated from the rest of the community (Borum and Philpot, 1993). If an officer has adopted an "us vs. them" attitude, he/she may be suspicious of other people's intentions and attempt to alienate the family from other people. The officer's suspiciousness and overprotectiveness may also prevent the family from making social contacts and developing personal support systems outside of the departmental boundaries. Hence, the police family may be coping with isolation and negative public perception. Additionally, the police officer often faces problems with role ambiguity.

Isolation

As previously stated, police officers often feel more comfortable among fellow officers (Vincent, 1990), as they feel others are unable to understand the complexities of their jobs. The suspicious and overprotective officer may not trust other people, including friends of his/her spouse, and may not want to socialise with them. This isolates the spouse from other social support networks and alienates him/her from the rest of society. Police officers' unwillingness to socialise with other people outside of the profession restricts the family from sharing experiences with other people unlike themselves. The result may be boredom and frustration for the spouse, as well as complete dependency on the officer to provide the social supports and social contacts. Lacking support systems of their own, spouses may feel lonely, depressed, and alienated from all other groups in society, even from their own family. If marriages break down, the spouse will likely be left with very little social support.

Police: Selected Issues

Even if police officers wanted to socialise with non-police families, shift work often prevents them from doing so. Activities have to be planned around the officer's schedule with no guarantee that the officer will be able to attend, as emergencies and arrests can detain him/her at work. Thus, it is often difficult for the police family to socialise with others on a regular or spontaneous basis.

Public perception

Police officers and their families often find themselves on public display, living in a type of "fish bowl" (Arahan, 1984). Most police officers are quite sensitive about their reputation and often feel the need to project an image of a strong individual who exercises complete control. The police officer may become anxious about the activities and behaviours of the spouse and family, and may set strict and unrealistic rules. Police officers may also become authoritarian and dogmatic in their approach to family problems (Nordlicht, 1979). Some police officers feel that others will think that if they cannot control the behaviour of their own family, they cannot be trusted to control the behaviour of the people in the community.

Additionally, the public often reacts ambivalently towards police officers, as they can be both needed and resented (Arahan, 1984; Nordlicht, 1979). Arahan (1984) suggests that the public respects and needs them, but they also resent and fear them. The public holds certain stereotypes of police officers that are quite conflicting. On the one hand, police officers are seen as defenders of truth and justice, and on the other, they are seen as "pigs" and "power mongers". This ambivalence and ambiguous attitude towards policing can be frustrating and demoralising for the officer.

Reiser (1978) also suggests that police wives are very much concerned about the public attitudes towards police officers and their families. Spouses are often forced to deal with stereotypes of police officers and to defend their husband's honor or choice of career. The wife may feel the need to be on her best behaviour when out in the community and this may also increase her anxiety. A study by Stenmark, et al. (1982) illustrates this point. Police officers' wives felt that the public expected police families to display flawless behaviour and obey laws to a greater extent than other families. They often felt they were forced to defend their husbands during discussions about police corruption, which they found stressful and intimidating.

122

Role ambiguity

Role ambiguity or role conflict generally occurs as a result of ambiguous public perceptions, family and work conflicts, and expectations. Researchers suggest that ambiguous roles and unpredictable expectations can greatly impair a person's overall abilities (Cox, 1996; Hageman, 1978).The varying roles that police officers are expected to play can often be confusing and difficult to change upon demand. This inability to "change hats" between work and home can create stress within the marriage. It is easy to imagine how difficult it would be for an authoritarian, controlling, and domineering police officer to quickly become a soft-hearted, tender, loving, compromising spouse. Bradstreet (1994) suggests that police work requires a vast number of responses to different situations. The role of the police officer is one of server, protector, law enforcer, psychologist, doctor, and saviour.

In contrast, when the officer returns home, the role is much less important and romantic. Officers continue to focus on their responsibility for the family, and often stay in their protective/provider mode. The officer strives to keep the home a safe haven, but in doing so, is unable to relax and enjoy the time spent with family. Unable to relax, the officer may prefer to spend time with police friends, where it is possible to relax and unwind. Inevitably, without physical closeness, emotional and psychological closeness cannot exist, and the marriage may suffer.

Hageman (1978) attempted to empirically investigate the association between role conflict in police officers and the quality of their marriage. The police uniform produces both negative and positive reactions from the public and the officer may become a target for public hostility, antagonism, and non-cooperation. The position of a law enforcement officer often includes more than one role. Hageman defines role conflict as being mutually exclusive demands resulting from the performance of two or more roles by any one actor. In other words, two or more groups in society placing different expectations on an individual, in which it would be impossible to fulfill all roles. Police officers often struggle between their occupational role and their marital role. Commanding and fellow officers often have expectations of an officer that are not congruent with the expectations of the spouse. For example, the commanding officer may expect the officer to commit 24 hours a day to the job, where spouse and family obviously expect the officer to devote part of his/her time to them.

Police wives have reported that the more their husbands

were away from the home, the less satisfying the marriage was. Hageman (1978) found that police officers who had been in the service for a long time had higher ratings of emotional repression and lower levels of marital satisfaction when compared to new recruits.

Conclusions

Overall, the quality of research examining the associations between police work and marital satisfaction is quite poor. To begin with, most of the literature to date has originated from the 70s and early 80s, questioning the validity of the relevance in the new millenium. Many of the recent papers simply recycle old ideas. Few empirically based studies have been conducted in this area, and much of what has been published is based on opinion, stereotypes, and clinical populations (typically the worse cases). It is therefore difficult to assess the true impact that police work has on a marriage today. It is quite possible, too, that there are newer issues that are more relevant to today's police officers. For example, very few papers/studies examine job stresses for women police officers and their non-police husbands. Similarly, community-based policing may decrease some of the problems outlined in this chapter, such as public ambiguity and perceptions of police officers, and even officer mistrust of the public.

Research in the United States (Gentz and Taylor, 1994) suggests that the majority of police officers surveyed believed that officers had a higher rate of divorce than the general public even though no significant differences were found between divorce rates in the police department and the general public. Police officers reported to the researchers that being a police officer had affected their own marital status in a negative way. Of the divorced officers, 68% believed that their career contributed to their divorce. The study suggests that officers perceive their careers as negatively impacting upon their marriage and that this perception may be partly contributing to marital conflict. Couples may project the blame onto the occupation and believe that police work negatively influences marriage.

There are a good many clues in the research literature as to factors in the police occupation that may negatively impact marriages. It is generally uncertain, however, even in traditional policing, whether or not police work negatively affects personal relationships to an extent greater than many other occupations.

Ten

The Future of Policing

Dennis Forcese

Introduction

What does the future hold for policing? In a sense, the past is the present, and the future is now. Policing as we know it has existed for about 170 years. It has, of course, changed over that time. There has been growth, technological change, amendments in recruit selection and training, altered response demands, and periodic public challenges. In this chapter, however, we select three themes as generally distinguishable over the years and into the future. These include: issues or tensions relating to the correct composition or personnel qualities of police services; the correct role and powers of police in civil democratic society; and, the boundaries of policing (and the state) in the face of global economics and global crime. The latter two issues are most obviously interrelated, but so too the outcomes are related to the quality of police personnel.

Police Personnel

The major change in police composition has been the increased participation of women in policing, a change, as discussed in Chapter Eight, that is still unfolding. Another visible change has been some discernible shift to higher education of police officers and police recruits, a trend that may be expected to continue. A major change objective that has failed, despite being on the map for at least two decades, is more diverse and representative ethnic representation, with an emphasis on visible minorities (Forcese, 1999:128-134). There can be little doubt that diversification, including probably some pressure for changed representation of police personnel by sexual preference, will feature in the years to come. The coming competition for employees as a wave of retirements affects the Canadian labour force over the next decade will probably oblige police, as well as other employers, to compete for immigrants as well as Canadian-born workers — and the immigrants are likely, in large numbers, to be visible minorities.

Canada's demographics are such that we will have an ageing population and only modest population growth, assuming replacement by immigration. Population maintenance, let alone growth, is not to be expected by natural increase through births, for the present Canadian birth rate is below replacement. Over the previous decade Canada has set high immigration levels, tending to increase overall population size, as well as to increase population heterogeneity. Perhaps the so-called "war on terrorism" (begun in the latter part of 2001) will moderate immigration intakes, but this is unlikely, for reasons of labour force need and economic growth. There is likely to be, even with sustained immigration levels, considerable competition for skilled employees — a competition in which police services must participate. Recruitment of quality personnel will become a major problem for services, especially as retirements remain at high levels with the exit of the large numbers of persons hired in the 1970s. Such recruitment, of course, is the basis of quality policing, for whatever the managerial and public controls, good policing will depend upon good personnel with well-honed skills. And the competition for personnel will push demands for improved compensation levels, further stressing the ability of police organisations to field adequate numbers of officers.

Police, perhaps, missed an opportunity to upgrade the educational qualifications and diversity of their personnel in the 1990s. By that decade it was clear that there was a recognition by young people that policing was an attractive employment, not just for lower middle-class Caucasians, but for university students, including members of minorities. At the same time, jobs, especially public sector jobs, were relatively scarce. With the new millennium, however, police now face — along with all other employers — a very competitive employment market. All sectors are seeking to renew personnel, and arguably the police no longer have a market edge, the "recession" of 2001–2002 notwithstanding.

In the wake of September 11, 2001, police already appear to be experiencing a labour shortage. Work demands have increased and police have taken up an historic complaint with a vengeance, declaring that they lack the manpower to do everything expected of them. A sharp illustration may be had from England, where the Scotland Yard commissioner revealed that there was a shortage of police on the streets as more police effort was diverted to counter-terrorism: "We have a problem balancing the demands of counter-terrorism and street crime." While announcing that untrained personnel, such as traffic wardens, would be used as patrol officers, a 40% increase over the previous year in street crime in London was also remarked (*Ottawa Citizen*, January 12, 2002).

In the rush to attend to terrorism, for example, officers have undoubtedly been diverted from other tasks, including the policing of drug trafficking. One report suggested that as many as 2000 RCMP officers had been reassigned from drug investigations to terrorism-related activities, some as banal as guard duties (*Globe and Mail*, October 26, 2001). So too, of course, in the United States, where the FBI abandoned investigations in order to pursue the terrorism priority (*New York Times*, October 28, 2001). Should the abandonment of fields of investigation such as drug trafficking be permanent, the trickle-down work load upon local police agencies will be significant.

Additionally, not unrelated to the terrorism concern, and exacerbating a manpower problem, many police services seem likely to experience increased difficulty in retaining personnel. Retirements are attractive (there were 375 retirees in Toronto in 2001), as are "different" police environments. Younger experienced officers will be competed for and may tend to leave less attractive policing environments. For example, the Toronto police reported losing 109 people to other services in 2001 (*Toronto Star*, April 5, 2002). Another illustration of the problem of employee retention may be taken from the United States. In New York City there is an accelerated rate of police retirement, with 3,776 officers, twice as many in 2001 as in 2000 who have retired. Approximately 20 per cent (807 officers) had less than five years of police service. Related to the salary pressure observation remarked above, New York City police lag behind other major jurisdictions in compensation levels, and arguably, too, the city is a relatively high-risk and high-tension policing area, especially when compared with suburban alternatives in policing as well as private sector opportunities. In seeking to stem this exodus the Police Commissioner, at time of writing, was seeking legislative authority to allow officers to draw down some retirement benefits while staying on the job (*New York Times*, January 14, 2002). A measure in response to personnel needs was announced in Toronto, where retired officers were being offered $30 per hour to patrol, answer 911 calls, and fill civilian jobs (*Toronto Star*, April 5, 2002). In Western Canada, the Edmonton Police Service indicated that they would do their utmost "to steal" trained officers from Calgary — a measure they considered reciprocal (*National Post*, April 5, 2002).

The competition will include not only other police services but also other organisations related to security. For example, should there be an increased standard for airport security, at the ground level and the supervisory level, another lucrative alternative to policing — among many others in the burgeoning area of private security — will exist. Such a demand will compound the "raiding" of police personnel by private sector security firms, which has already been a growth area in the North American economy for decades. In the United States, for example, it appears that the Department of Transportation will seek airport security directors at one of the highest salaries in the public sector, up to US$150,000 — with an emphasis on candidates with experience in law enforcement (*New York Times*, January 13, 2002).

At the same time in Canada and in the States, there is some reason to perceive wastage in trained police personnel. Early retirements, at all levels, deprive the police and the public of people in whom some investment has been made. Embedded in contracts are practices and assumptions that fix a relatively short career span for police as contrasted to other occupations. Consider as illustrative — also related to the unattractiveness of some policing environments — that in the Liverpool area of Britain, 77% of Merseyside officers "retire prematurely on medical grounds with enhanced pensions." Generally in Britain "nearly one third of all officers retire on medical grounds and half of all officers retire early, at an estimated cost to the taxpayer of more than $1.45 billion (USD)," an estimate that suggests problem likely to increase into the future (*The Economist*, December 22, 2001, p. 72). When exits are additionally encouraged by "buy-outs," as a fix for apparent internal management problems, often associated with the appointment of a new chief, the waste seems all the more evident. Similarly, when chiefs are hounded from office by employee groups or by interfering local politicians the cost to the public of a scarce human resource is noteworthy. When chiefs of police, or their deputies, exit policing while in their 50s, perhaps serving only one full term or less in office, and a succeeding chief purges the organisation of the "old guard" and possible rivals, there seems some breakdown in orderly career and organisational development and a discarding of the management experience and skills that one assumes led to the appointments in the first instance — the result is wastage.

Public Role of the Police

Issues relating to the role of policing in the past, present, and into the future may be summarised as relating to two contrasting tendencies in policing. One may be distinguished as between the pro-active intentions of the founders of Anglo-American policing, as exemplified by Peel, and the reactive practices of police inherent in the paramilitary organisational structure and the steering effect of daily public demands. This major matter has been featured in the previous emphasis in chapters considering the implications of community policing. A second contradiction is that between the police as agents of the public, with constrained delegated powers as again conceived of ideally in the Peel model, and the police as organisations and as individuals seeking extensions of power in aid of their emphasis on law enforcement but also in the interests of police organisations and personnel. These are closely related, of course, and fundamentally express an ongoing tension and equilibrium process in democratic societies.

Canadian policing has evolved with the Canadian democratic nation state. Indeed, as we have argued, policing contributed to the nature and stability of the Canadian democracy. Problems and criticisms aside, policing continues to do so even as the traditional legitimacy of police services is at risk, and in need of continuous re-affirmation, as may be inferred from Toronto circumstances related in Chapter 6. Police actions, including enforcement choices and emphases, help shape social norms and values: so too do Canadian values — perhaps especially a wish for and a pride in peace and order — shape policing. There remains by and large an affirmative interaction between Canadians and the police even as there are disquieting challenges. One measure is the consistent support shown police by the Canadian public as measured by opinion polls. A poll by Leger Marketing (December 18, 2001) reported a national satisfaction rating with municipal police of 79.8 per cent. The rating in Ontario was 81.6 per cent, and in Quebec it was 81.6 per cent while nationally for the RCMP the satisfaction level was 81.7 per cent (*Toronto Star*, January 6, 2002).

Yet the persisting role of police is expressed in a democratic society that is also characterised by persisting inequalities. Police, therefore, in their lawful interventions, are invariably placed in opposition to some number of individuals seeking social change, as well as those more likely to commit highly visible infractions by virtue of stressed economic circumstance. Youth and the working class, especially minorities, are more likely to encounter the "iron fist" of policing as contrasted with the "velvet glove." Even as Canadians still approve of their police, they do distinguish problems in policing, as when 28.8 per cent of Canadians considered that police discriminate against minorities (*Toronto Star*, January 6, 2002).

Generally, too, there is a concern that police are too intrusive, as in information gathering and surveillance. Consider, for example, that even as community policing is generally viewed as reform-oriented and community-responsive and accountable, there are critics who consider such a policing style to be an enhanced manifestation of police information gathering (Ericson and Haggerty, 1997). Into the future, community policing aside, there will undoubtedly be tension between police surveillance techniques and civil libertarians. The activities of undercover officers will be one such area of tension, as legislation now explicitly permits police illegalities without judicial authorisation. But additionally, technological approaches to surveillance will be employed and challenged, such as video surveillance. In British Columbia the provincial Privacy Commissioner ruled that the RCMP uses of video surveillance of public spaces violates privacy rights. Used as a tool to control a high-crime area, the RCMP has discontinued taping but persists in continuous monitoring of the cameras (*Toronto Star*, January 8, 2002). Subsequently, in Hamilton, Ontario, working to guidelines of the Ontario Privacy Commissioner, municipal police are initiating video surveillance of downtown areas — acceptable to the Commissioner if the surveillance does not encroach into private areas, such as windows. Cameras are also in use in Sudbury and London, Ontario, and the Toronto police — Canada's largest municipal jurisdiction — have announced similar intention. Such camera use is related to an aspect of community policing: the use of volunteers. Non-police personnel may be used for the video monitoring (*Toronto* Star, January 8, 2002).

Events, too, have intervened, particularly September 11, 2001, as well as various attempts to control protests at meetings of world leaders. Military-style and forceful policing have been conspicuous, so much so that in one instance, following the Ottawa meeting of the G-20 in November 2001, the chief of police was prompted to deny that police actions had harmed community policing in the city (CBC, December 3, 2001). Consequent from September 11, an inevitable resort to ethnic profiling was recognised by some police as an explicit threat to community policing initiatives. In the United States the chief of police of Seattle, having refused to cooperate with the FBI in its efforts to interview men of Middle Eastern backgrounds, remarked that "we don't want to harm relationships with community members that we have worked hard for years to build" (*New York Times*, November 21, 2001). The sentiments were echoed by other American municipal chiefs (*New York Times*, November 22, 2001). Similarly, there is an even more blatant threat to community policing: the prospect of simply abandoning community initiatives in order to attach personnel to other response demand areas; crime prevention will again yield to short-term demands (*New York Times*, October 28, 2001).

Perhaps also damaging police community initiatives, municipal chiefs were remarking upon a "disconnect between federal and local law enforcement" (*New York Times*, November 22, 2001). With all local authorities exercised over possible threats to their communities, American chiefs of police meeting in Toronto demanded more effective information-sharing with intelligence agencies (*Ottawa Citizen*, October 29, 2001). Municipal chiefs of police considered themselves out of the loop, perhaps a perception that had only been dramatised by the events of September 11, 2001.

Again, as an outcome of those events, the pressure on Parliament to strengthen policing powers was considerable. New legislation introduced was also oriented to a pre-terrorist priority — organised crime. The government of Canada (and those of the United States and United Kingdom) hastened to legislate and endorse more intrusive police powers after September 11. The legislation was generally seen to threatened constitutional rights in each society, even as a majority of the public hastened to support such measures, given the widespread fears of terrorism. One significance of the Canadian legislation was to be found in what appears much like a return to policing's past when illegally obtained evidence was accepted by Canadian courts, as legislation provides for the police to break criminal laws without judicial authorisation: only the approval of a senior police officer is required. Wiretapping powers were also extended, as well as RCMP access to personal information on domestic and international flights (*Globe and Mail*, May 2, 2002). Other measures generally expanded police powers of detention, surveillance, and search and seizure. Both criminals and terrorists now could be caught up in provisions regarding associating with criminal organisations (*National Post*, December 22, 2001).

In North America, initiated by the U.S. Congress (*Globe and Mail*, October 26, 2001) and following opposition pressure in Canada, a "sunset" clause was introduced in legislation, providing for expiry or explicit renewal of anti-terrorism provisions in three years. Police spokespersons publicly lobbied for no further weakening, assuring that the measures would only be invoked in special circumstances and there would be no police abuse of rights (CBC Radio News, December 5, 2001).

Ironically, even as elements of the public are concerned at expanded police powers, albeit generally in favour, the legislation does not satisfy all police, nor bridge the rift between management and employee groups in policing. Police subsequently complained, through the auspices of the Canadian Police Association, that "police currently do not have enough manpower to fight both organised crime and terrorism" (CBC Radio News, January 7, 2002). Later, however, meeting in Ottawa at a counter-terrorism workshop, chiefs acknowledged that the new powers had yet to be implemented and were sufficient to police needs (*Toronto Star*, January 19, 2002). As remarked by the RCMP Commissioner, also contradicting the musings of the newly named Justice Minister, the laws "are sufficient for us to act" (*Ottawa Citizen*, January 18, 2002; *Toronto Star*, January 19, 2002).

Transnational Policing

The conventional experience of international policing has been best expressed in the so-called war on drugs. Additionally, there has been some explicit concern with policing financial crimes, in a circumstance of global economies as well as the flow of proceeds from organised crime. Preoccupation with biker gangs has obviously been an attempt to cope with transnational organised crime of a low-grade level, and of course, was an example of successful police lobbying and publicity in achieving desired legislation. Enforcement priorities, such as bikers and drugs, increasingly require international police liaison.

Such liaison is defended as being part of the modern evolution of policing in the face of "globalisation" and "transnational financial networks" (*National Post*, December 22, 2001). Reinforced by the interest in financing of terrorism, police participation in multi-agency bodies will inevitably be of some emphasis in the future of Canada's police. Illustrative is the Financial Transactions and Reports Analysis Section (FINTRAC), involving the RCMP, federal government departments such as Canada Customs and also Citizenship and Immigration, as well as private-sector parties such as the Canadian Bankers Association (*Globe and Mail*, October 26, 2001). There is no reason to expect such demands to diminish in

the future, and perhaps especially, related to international terrorism, integrated police teams will come to be normal features. Such
joint teams as institutionalised rather than ad hoc police features
might especially come to characterise Canada–U.S. relations. From
the outset, for example, FINTRAC was described as "liaising with
the U.S. Federal Bureau of Investigation and other international
organisations" (*Globe and Mail*, October 26, 2001).

The world and its politics have intruded upon Canada and
domestic policing. The policing of meetings in Quebec City and
in Ottawa visibly brought to public view the fragile boundaries
of democracy, and oft-conflicting public rights of commerce, as-
sembly, and protests. Much as policing union demonstrations had
historically tested the limits and tactics of policing, the demands
attendant upon controlling international consultations and international public objections to global trade practices generated new
levels of consultation and collaboration not just between the state
and its police, but among police agencies domestically and inter-
nationally. Additionally, police, in collaboration with other state
regulatory bodies, found themselves dealing not only with their
own citizens and organisations but also with foreign nationals.
Such experiences, in conjunction with September 11 and consequent legislation, have in fact blurred the definitions of tolerable
protest, illegalities, and terrorism—a whole new normative set
needs to evolve in the near future.

Yet, while legislation has been passed apparently enhanc-
ing a police role, it must ever be borne in mind that the courts
exist to interpret legislation. Coincident with the police powers
being demanded to combat terrorism, for example, the Supreme
Court of Canada handed down two unanimous decisions relating
to police undercover procedures (arising from "sting" operations),
decisions that police perceive as limiting their investigative capacities. Essentially the decisions held that in the interests of "public scrutiny," details of police tactics can be published (CBC Radio
News, November 15, 2001) and that publication bans must be limited to exceptional circumstances (*Ottawa Citizen*, November 16,
2001). One Justice wrote: "The improper use of bans ... seriously
deprives the Canadian public of its ability to know of and be able
to respond to police practices that, left unchecked, could erode
the fabric of Canadian society and democracy" (*Ottawa Citizen*,
November 16, 2001). The test put by the Court for publication
bans referred to a circumstance of "a serious threat to the proper
administration of justice" (*Ottawa Citizen*, November 16, 2001).

On an affirmative note, there is an intriguing aspect of international policing that is perhaps rather more to Canada's taste. Relatively modest experiences to date of Canadian police, both RCMP and municipal officers, serving abroad in Bosnia, Haiti, or East Timor, are illustrative of what promises to be an increased emphasis upon international public order with a civil regulatory body. To cite but one example, suggesting a particular role for senior officers in such off-shore policing, late in 2001 the United Nations named a senior RCMP officer, with previous experience in Haiti and Africa, to head a force of 1,500 police officers from 40 nations in East Timor (CBC Radio News, November 23, 2001). Such activities suggest the prospect, harking back to Chapter One, of Canada's police as an exportable resource, adept in the delicate art of democratic policing.

Conclusions

The new millennium roared in with a major challenge to Canadian conceptions of safety, the limits of freedom, and the responsibilities of governments.. Street demonstrations and terrorism, relatively unfamiliar to this generation of Canadians, underlined the historic challenge of policing in a democratic society. The proper balance between state/police intervention, collective rights, and individual rights have ever been the crux of democratic policing, but perhaps never more evidently so as after September 11, 2001. In the immediate future the values inherent in traditional Canadian policing, stressing a detached and politically neutral objectivity, merged with the values or philosophy of a community-based style, stressing partnerships, communications, and a sensitivity to diversity, seem all the more in need of vigorous and vigilant maintenance and renewal.

References

Adamson, Raymond. 1987. "Police force communication: Member perceptions." *Canadian Police College Journal* 10:233-272.

Adamson, Raymond, and Gene Deszca. 1990. "Police force communications: Managing meaning on the firing line." *Canadian Police College Journal* 14:155-171.

Alexander, D.A. 1994. "The impact of police work on police officers spouses and families." In T. Reese and E. Scrivner, eds., *Law Enforcement Families*. US Department of Justice, FBI.

Alexander, D.A., and L.G. Walker. 1996. "The perceived impact of police work on police officers' spouses and families." *Stress Medicine*, 12:239-246.

Allard, C. 1989. "Ont. policewoman loses pregnancy discrimination suit." *The Lawyers Weekly* (January).

Alvaro, Sam. 2000. Tactical Law Enforcement in Canada: An exploratory survey of Canadian police agencies. Master's thesis, Carleton University, Ottawa.

Angell, John E. 1975. "Organizing Police For the Future: An update of the democratic model." *Criminal Justice Review* 1:35-52.

Arahan, C.H. 1984. "A policeman's life and marital problems." RCMP *Gazette* 46(10):13-16.

Bayley, David H. 1991. *Managing the Future: Prospective Issues in Canadian Policing*. Ottawa: Ministry of the Solicitor General.

Beehr, T.A., and J.E. Newman. 1978. "Job stress, employee health, and organisational effectiveness: A facet analysis model and literature review." *Personnel Psychology* 31:665-699.

Bell, P. 1977. "Measuring up to force called discriminatory." *The Globe and Mail* 29 September.

Bobier, Paul. 2000. "Politics and Policing," *Municipal World* (November):3-4.

Borum, R., and C. Philpot. 1993. "Therapy with law enforcement couples: Clinical management of the 'high risk lifestyle'." *The American Journal of Family Therapy* 21:122-135.

Bradstreet, R. 1994. "Cultural hurdles to healthy families." In T. Reese and E. Scrivner, eds., *Law Enforcement Families*. US Department of Justice, FBI.

Police: Selected Issues

Braiden, Chris. 1986. "Community policing — a personal view." In Donald Loree and Chris Murphy (eds.), *Community Policing in the 1980's: Recent advances in police programs*. Ottawa: Solicitor General of Canada.

Burke, R.J. 1988. "Some antecedents and consequences of work-family conflict." *Journal of Social Behaviour and Personality* 3:287-302.

Calgary Police Service. 1977. Annual Report. Calgary: The Service.

Canadian Center for Justice Statistics (CCJS). 1995. *Juristat*. Ottawa: Statistics Canada.

Canadian Center for Justice Statistics (CCJS). 1997. Police Personnel and Expenditures in Canada — 1997. Ottawa: Statistics Canada.

———. 1999. Police Personnel and Expenditures in Canada — 1999. Ottawa: Statistics Canada.

Cherry, T.M., and D. Lester. 1979. "An exploratory study of police officers' satisfaction in marriage." *Psychological Reports* 43(3).

Clairmont, Donald. 1990. *To the Forefront: Community-Based Zone Policing in Halifax*. Ottawa: Canadian Police College.

Cordner, Gary W. 1978. "Open and Closed Models of Police Organizations: Traditions, Dilemmas and Practical Considerations." *Journal of Police Science and Administration* 6:22-34.

Cox, S.M. 1996. *Police: Practices, perspectives, problems*. Boston: Allyn and Bacon.

Ericson, Richard. 1981. *Making Crime: A Study of Detective Work*. Toronto: Butterworths Canada.

———. 1989. "Patrolling the facts: Secrecy and publicity in police work." *British Journal of Sociology* 40:205-226.

Ericson, Richard, and Kevin Haggerty. 1997. *Policing the Risk Society*. Toronto: University of Toronto Press.

Ericson, Richard, Kevin Haggerty, and Kevin Carriere. 1993. "Community policing as communications policing." In Dieter Dolling and Thomas Feltes, eds., *Community Policing: Comparative Aspects of Community Oriented Police Work*. Holzkirchen: Felix-Verlag, pp. 37-70.

Feminist Majority Foundation. 1999. "Equality Denied: The Status of Women in Policing." [avail. on-line at: http://www.womenandpolicing.org/status1998.html].

Forcese, Dennis. 1980. "Police unionism: Employee-management relations in Canadian police forces." *Canadian Police College Journal* 4:79-129.

———. 1999. "Police unions." In Dennis Forcese, ed., *Policing Canadian Society*. Rev. ed. Scarborough: Prentice-Hall Allyn and Bacon Canada, pp. 102-121.

Forcese, Dennis, ed. 1999. *Policing Canadian Society*. Rev. ed. Scarborough: Prentice-Hall Allyn and Bacon Canada. [originally published 1992]

Ford. P. 1995. "Community Policing and SWAT: Still Trying to Make Friends." *The Tactical Edge* (Spring).

Friedmann, Robert, 1992. *Community Policing: Comparative perspectives and prospects*. New York: St. Martin's Press.

References

Galloway, Robert, and Laurie Fitzgerald. 1992. "Service quality in policing." *FBI Law Enforcement Bulletin* (Nov.):1-7.

Gandz, Jeffrey. 1990. "The employee empowerment era." *Business Quarterly* (Autumn):74-79.

Gentz, D., and D. Taylor. 1994. "Marital status and attitudes about divorce among veteran law enforcement." In T. Reese and E. Scrivner, eds., *Law Enforcement Families*. US Department of Justice, FBI.

Germann, A.C. 1971. "Changing the Police — The Impossible Dream?" *Journal of Criminal Law, Criminology and Police Science* 62:416-421.

Goldstein, Herman. 1990. *Problem-oriented policing*. New York: McGraw-Hill.

Greene, J.R., and S.D. Mastrofski, eds. 1988. *Community Policing: Rhetoric or Reality*. New York: Praeger.

Greene, J.R., and R.B. Taylor. 1988. "Community-based policing and foot patrol: Issues of theory and evaluation." In J.R. Greene and S.D. Mastrofski, eds., *Community Policing: Rhetoric or Reality*. New York: Praeger, pp. 195-224.

Grosman, Brian. 1975. *Police Command*. Toronto: Macmillan.

Guyot, Dorothy. 1977. "Bending Granite: Attempts to Change the Rank Structure of American Police Departments." *Journal of Police Service and Administration* 7:253-284.

Hageman, M.J. 1978. "Occupational stress and marital relationships." *Journal of Police Science and Administration* 6:402-411.

Hale, Edward B. 1974. *The Task Force on Policing in Ontario: Report to the Solicitor Genera*. Toronto: Solicitor General of Ontario.

Hart, P.M., A.J. Wearing, and B. Heady. 1995. "Police stress and well being: Integrating personality, coping, and daily work experiences." *Journal of Occupational and Organisational Psychology*, 68:133-156.

Hattery, A.J., and R.G. Merrill. 1997. "The impact of non-day and non-overlapping shift work on child development and marital quality: A preliminary analysis." Paper given at a meeting of the American Sociological Association.

Haydon, Arthur. 1973. *The Riders of the Plains*. Edmonton: Hurtig. [originally published 1910]

Heidensohn, F. 1994. " We Can Handle it out Here: Women Officers in Britain and the USA and the Policing of Public Order." *Policing and Society* 4.

Hirsch, Werner Z. 1959. "Expenditure Implications of Metropolitan Growth and Consolidation." *Review of Economics and Statistics* 41.

Horne, David. 1993. "Public opinion surveys: Implications for police organizations." *Canadian Police College Journal* 16:263-281.

Horn, Jo. 1991. "The future of crime prevention: Inter-agency issues." In Donald Loree and Robert Walker, eds., *Community Crime Prevention: Shaping the Future*. Ottawa: Minister of Supply and Services Canada, pp. 115-136.

Hornick, J.P., B.A. Burrows, D.M. Phillips, and B.N. Leighton. 1991. "An impact evaluation of the neighbourhood foot patrol program." *Canadian Journal of Program Evaluation* 6:47-70.

Hornick, Joseph, Barbara Burrows, Donna Phillips, and Barry Leighton. 1993.

"An impact evaluation of the Edmonton Neighborhood Foot Patrol Program." In James Chacko and Stephen Nancoo, eds., *Evaluating Justice: Canadian Policies and Programs.* Toronto: Thompson Educational Publishing.

Hornick, J.P., B.A. Burrows, I. Tjosvold, and D.M. Phillips. 1990. *An Evaluation of the Neighbourhood Foot Patrol Program of Edmonton Police Service.* Ottawa: Ministry of the Solicitor General Canada.

Hornick, J.P., B.N. Leighton, and B.A. Burrows. 1993. "Evaluating community policing: The Edmonton project." In Julian Roberts and Joe Hudson, eds., *Evaluating Justice: Canadian Policies and Programs.* Toronto: Thompson Educational Publishing, pp. 61-92.

Huey, John. 1991. "Nothing impossible." *Fortune* (Sept. 23), pp. 134-140.

Janson, Robert, and Richard Gunderson. 1990/91. "The team approach to company wide change." *National Productivity Review* (Winter):35-44.

Jones, Sandra. 1986. *Policewomen and equality formal policy v. informal practice?.* Basingstoke, U.K.: Macmillan.

Kelling, George. 1978. "Police Field Services and Crime: The presumed Effects of Capacity." *Crime and Delinquency* 24:173-183.

Kennedy, Leslie W. 1991. "The evaluation of community-based policing in Canada." *Canadian Police College Journal* 15:275-289.

Koenig, Daniel. 1991. *Do Police Cause Crime?* Ottawa: Canadian Police College.

Kraska, P. 1994. "The Police and the Military in the Post War Era." *Police Forum* 4.

Kraska, P. 1996. "Enjoying Militarism: Poltical/Personal Dilemmas in Studying U.S. Police Paramilitary Units." *Justice Quarterly* 13.

Kraska, P., and F. Cubellis. 1997. "Militarizing Mayberry and Beyond: Making Sense of American Paramilitary Policing." *Justice Quarterly* 4.

Kraska, P., and V. Kappeler V. 1997. "Militarizing American Police: The Rise and Normalization of Paramilitary Units." *Social Problems* 44.

Kratcoski, Peter and Duane Dukes, eds. 1995. *Issues in Community Policing.* Cincinnati: Anderson Publishing.

Kroes, W.H., B. Margolis, and J. Hurrel. 1974. "Job stresses in policemen." *Journal of Police Science and Administration* 2(2).

Leighton, Barry and Marsha Mitzak, eds. 1991. *Community Policing: Shaping the Future.* Ottawa and Toronto: Solicitor General of Canada and Ministry of the Solicitor General Ontario.

Lewis-Horne, N. 2001. Connecting the Gender Division of Labour in Policing to the Construction of Femininity in Police Work. Ph.D. dissertation, Carleton University, Ottawa.

Lipset, S.M. 1963. *The First New Nation: The United States in historical and comparative perspective.* New York: Norton.

——. 1990. *Continental Divide: The values and institutions of the United States and Canada..* New York: Routledge.

Loney, Martin. 1977. "A polictical economy of citizen participation." In Leo Panitch, ed., *The Canadian State: Political economy and political power.* Toronto: University of Toronto Press.

References

Lunney, Robert. 1989. "The role of the police leader in the 21st century." In Donald Loree, ed., *Future Issues in Policing: Symposium Proceedings*. Ottawa: Canadian Police College, pp. 197-213.

Macko, S. 1997. "SWAT: Is it being used too much?" *Emergency Services Reports* (July).

MacLagan, Patrick. 1987. "Resistance to Organisational Development in a Police Force: A Case Study." *Police Studies* 60:303-312.

Marson, Brian. 1991. "Making participative leadership work." In James McDavid and Brian Marson, eds., *Well Performing Government Organisations*. Ottawa. Canadian Institute of Public Administration.

Maynard, P.E., and N.E. Maynard. 1982. "Stress in police families: Some policy implications." *Journal of Police Science and Administration* 10:302-314.

Maynard, P., N.E. Maynard, H. McCubbin, and D. Shao. 1980. "Family life and the police profession: Coping patterns wives employ in managing job stress and the family environment." *Family Relations* 29:495-501.

McElroy, Jerome, Colleen Cosgrove, and Susan Sadd. 1993. *Community Policing: The CPOP in New York*. Newbury Park: Sage.

Miller, Susan L. 1999. *Gender and Community Policing: Walking the Talk*. Boston: Northeastern University Press.

Miller, Linda S., and Kären M. Hess. 1994. *Community policing: Theory and practice*. Minneapolis/St. Paul: West Publishing.

Moore, Mark Harrison. 1992. "Problem-solving and community policing." In Michael Tonry and Norval Morris, eds., *Modern Policing*. Chicago: University of Chicago Press, pp. 99-158.

Morris, Nancy. 1997. Community Policing from a Participant Observer's Perspective. Master's thesis, Norwich University, Vermont.

Moses Schulz, D. 1993. "Policewomen in the 1950s: Paving the Way for Patrol." *Women and Criminal Justice* 4(2).

Murphy, Chris. 1986. The Social and Formal Organization of Small Town Policing. Ph.D. dissertation, University of Toronto.

Naeve, Edwin H., Edward R. Petersen, and B. William Simms. 1982. "An information processing model of police." *Canadian Police College Journal* 6:125-153.

Neiderhoffer, A. and E. Neiderhoffer. 1978. *From station house to ranch house*. Lexington, Mass.: Lexington Book.

Nicholas, W. 1973. "Policeman's family life feels the strain." *The Charlotte Observer*, 1 Dec. 1.

Nicoletti, J. and K. Spooner. 1994. "The effects of shift work on circadian rhythm desychronization and stress levels on law enforcement families." In T. Reese and E. Scrivner, eds., *Law Enforcement Families*. US Department of Justice, FBI.

Nordlicht, S. 1979. "Effects of stress on the police officer and family." *New York State Journal of Medicine* 79:400-401.

Normandeau, André, and Barry Leighton. 1990. *A Vision of the Future of Policing in Canada*: Ottawa: Solicitor General of Canada.

Police: Selected Issues

Ontario. 1993. *Police Services Act*. Toronto: Queen's Printer for Ontario.
——. 1994. *Community Policing Series: Shaping the Future*. Minister of the Solicitor General and Correctional Services. Toronto: Queen's Printer for Ontario.
Ontario. Ontario Police Commission. 1989. *Drinkwalter Report: Inquiry into Ontario Police Tactical Units*. Toronto: Ontario Police Commission. [issued as appendix C of Review of tactical units]
Ostrom, Elinor, and Roger B. Parks. 1973. "Suburban Police Departments: Too Many and Too Small." In Louis H. Massotti and Jeffrey K. Hadden, eds., *Urban Affairs Annual Reviews*, Vol. 7: *The Urbanization of the Suburbs*. Beverly Hills: Sage, pp. 367–402.
Ostrom, E., Roger B. Parks, and Gordon P. Whitaker. 1978a. *Patterns of Metropolitan Policing*. Cambridge, Mass.: Ballinger.
Ostrom, E., Roger B. Parks, and Gordon P. Whitaker. 1978b. "Some Evidence on the Effects of Police Agency Size" *Police Studies* 1:34–46.
Panitch, Leo. 1977. "The role and nature of the Canadian state." In Leo Panitch, ed., *The Canadian State: Political economy and political power*. Toronto: University of Toronto Press, pp. 3–27.
Peak, Ken, Robert Bradshaw, and Ronald Glensor. 1992. "Improving citizen perceptions of the police: 'Back to basics' with a community policing strategy." *Journal of Criminal Justice* 20:25–40.
Peak, Kenneth J., and Ronald W. Glensor. 1996. *Community Policing and Problem Solving: Strategies and Practices*. Englewood Cliffs, N.J.: Prentice-Hall.
Piotrowski, C.S. 1979. *Work and family*. New York: Free Press.
Podgorecki, Adam. 1995. *The Impersonality of Law and the Clash of Legal Cultures*. Ottawa: Carleton University, Department of Sociology and Anthropology Working Papers, v. 95-01.
Radelet, Louis and David Carter. 1994. *The Police and the Community*. 5th ed. Englewood Cliffs, N.J.: Prentice-Hall.
Reiser, M. 1973. "Police officers wives." In *Practical Psychology for police officers*. Springfield, IL: Charles C. Thomas.
Reiser, M. 1978. "The problems of police officers wives". *The Police Chief* (April), 38–42.
Roach, Lawrence T. 1986. "Implementing community based policing in the London Metropolitan Police." In Donald Loree and Chris Murphy (eds.), *Community Policing in the 1980's: Recent advances in police programs*. Ottawa: Solicitor General of Canada, pp. 75–95
Roberg, R.R. and J. Kuykendall. 1993. *Police and Society*. Belmont, CA: Wadsworth.
Sandler, Georgette Bennett, and Ellen Mintz. 1974. "Police Organizations: Their Changing Internal and External Relationships." *Journal of Police Science and Administration* 2:458–463.
Sauve, Robert. 1977. *Community Involvement in Criminal Justice: Report of the Task Force on the Role of the Private Sector in Criminal Justice*. Ottawa: Ministry of the Solicitor General Canada.
Schwartz, Alfred I., and Sumner N. Clarren. 1977. *The Cincinnati Team*

References

Policing Experiment. Washington, D.C.: Police Federation.

Seagrave, Jayne. 1992. "Community policing and the need for police research skills training." *Canadian Police College Journal* 16:204-211.

Serry, K. 1995. "Troop 17: 1974-1975. The RCMP's first women members are members first." *The Pony Express* (Oct.).

Sewell, John. 1985. *Police: Urban policing in Canada.* Toronto: Lorimer.

Sherman, Lawrence W. 1975. "Middle Management and Police Democratization: A reply to John E. Angell." *Criminology* 12:363-377.

Slaughter, C.S. 2000. "Historical Administration of Law: Women's Journey into Policing." Unpublished paper.

Sparrow, Malcolm, Mark Moore, and David Kennedy. 1990. *Beyond 911: A New Era for Policing.* New York: Basic Books.

Staines, G.L., and J.H. Pleck. 1983. *The impact of work schedules on the family.* Ann Arbour: University of Michigan, Institute for Social Research, Survey Research Center.

Statistics Canada. 2000. *Women in Canada 2000: A gender-based statistical report.* Ottawa. Minister of Industry.

Stenmark, D.E., L.C. DePiano, J.H. Wackwitz, C.D. Cannon, and S. Walfish. 1982. "Wives of police officers: Issues related to family job satisfaction and job longevity." *Journal of Police Science and Administration* 10:229-234.

Stevens, D. 1999. "Police Tactical Units and Community Response." *Law and Order.*

Stratton, J.G., 1975. "Pressures in law enforcement marriages: Some considerations." *The Police Chief* (Nov.), 44-47.

Super, J. 1995. "Psychological Characteristics of Successful SWAT/Tactical Response Team Personnel." *Journal of Police and Criminal Psychology* 10.

Territo, L., and H.J. Vetter. 1981. *Stress and police personnel.* Boston: Allyn and Bacon.

Terry, W.C. 1981. "Police stress: The empirical evidence." *Journal of Police Science and Administration* 9:61-75.

Tiebout, Charles, M. 1960. "Economies of Scale and Metropolitan Governments." *Review of Economics and Statistics* 42.

Tremblay, Pierre, and Claude Rochon. 1991. "D'une police efficace à une police informée : Lignes directrices d'un programme global de traitement de l'information." *Canadian Journal of Criminology* 33:407-420.

Trojanowicz, Robert. 1986. "Neighborhood Foot Patrol: The Flint, Michigan Experience." In Don Loree and Chris Murphy, eds., *Community Policing in the 1980's.* Ottawa: Canadian Police College.

Van Maanen, John and Ralph Katz. 1979. "Police perceptions of their work environment." *Sociology of Work and Occupations* 6:31-58.

Vincent, C. 1990. *Police Officer.* Ottawa: Carleton University Press.

Voydonoff, P. 1987. *Work and family life.* Newbury Park: Sage.

Walker, Christopher, and Gail Walker. 1989. *The Victoria Community Police Stations: An Exercise in Innovation.* Ottawa: Canadian Police College.

Walker, Gail, Christopher Walker, and James McDavid. 1992. *The Victoria Community Police Stations: A Three-Year Evaluation.* Ottawa: Canadian Police College.

Wasson, David K. 1975. *Community-Based Preventive Police: A Review.* Ottawa: Solicitor General of Canada.

Watson, N.A., and J.W. Sterling. 1969. *Police and their Opinions.* Gaithersburg: International Association of Chiefs of Police.

Webber, Alan M. 1991. "Crime and Management: An Interview with New York City Police Commissioner Lee P. Brown." *Harvard Business Review* (May–June):111–126.

Weber, Max. 1947. *The Theory of Social and Economic Organization.* New York: The Free Press.

Wilgus, Alan. 1991. "Forging change in spite of adversity." *Personnel Journal* (Sept.):60–67.

Wilson, James Q. 1978. *Varieties of Police Behavior.* Cambridge, Mass.: Harvard University Press.

Wilson, James Q., and George Kelling. "Broken Windows." *The Atlantic Monthly* (March):38–45.

The Golden Dog Press

This volume was produced using the TeX typesetting system, and Lucida Bright fonts.